IRON FLEET

IRON FLEET

The Great Lakes in World War II

George J. Joachim

Wayne State University Press   Detroit

GREAT LAKES BOOKS

A complete listing of the books in this series can be found at the back of this volume.

Philip P. Mason, Editor
Department of History, Wayne State University

Dr. Charles K. Hyde, Associate Editor
Department of History, Wayne State University

Library of Congress Cataloging-in-Publication Data

Joachim, George J.
    Iron fleet : the Great Lakes in World War II / George J. Joachim.
        p.   cm. — (Great Lakes books)
    Includes bibliographical references and index.
    ISBN 0-8143-2479-7 (alk. paper)
    1. Shipping—Great Lakes. 2. Iron mines and mining—Great Lakes
Region.   3. Raw materials—Government policy—United States.
4. World War, 1939–1945—Economic aspects—United States.
I. Title.   II. Series.
HE630.G7J6   1994
386'244'097709044—dc20   93-31205

Designer: Mary Primeau

Contents

Acknowledgments

I wish to express my appreciation to Ed Baganz, Bob Burns, Hubert Kessel, Perry Klumph, John LeCorn, Luke Manion, and Clarence McTevia, veterans of the war years on the lakes, for graciously sharing their time and memories. I also wish to thank Bob Graham, Jay Martin, and Susan Riggs of the Institute for Great Lakes Research for their kindness and invaluable assistance, and Doug Fiorani and Gary Rutowski for their technical advice. Lastly, but most importantly, thanks to my wife Sharon for her patience and support.

Abbreviations

COTP	Captain of the Port
IGLR	Institute for Great Lakes Research
LCA	Lake Carriers Association
LCI	Landing Craft, Infantry
LCP(L)	Landing Craft Personnel, Large
LCP(R)	Landing Craft Personnel, Ramped
LCVP	Landing Craft Vehicle and Personnel
LVC	Lake Vessel Committee of Lake Carriers Association
MC	U.S. Maritime Commission
MESR	*Marine Engineering and Shipping Review*
NDAC	National Defense Advisory Committee
NLRB	National Labor Relations Board
NMU	National Maritime Union
NSC	Newspaper Scrapbook Collection
ODT	Office of Defense Transportation
OPA	Office of Price Administration
OPD	Operations Division, U.S. Army
OPM	Office of Production Management
RG	Record Group (National Archives)
RMO	Recruitment and Manning Office
SPAB	Supply Priorities and Allocation Board
USES	U.S. Employment Service
USO	United Service Organizations
WLB	War Labor Board
WM	Wilson Marine
WMC	War Manpower Commission
WPB	War Production Board
WPD	War Plans Division
WSA	War Shipping Administration

Introduction

Perhaps there once was a time when courage, daring, imagination and intelligence were the hinges on which wars turned. No longer. The total wars of modern history give the decision to the side with the biggest factories. The economically inferior may win battles; they do not win all out wars.

—Geoffrey Perrett

World War II was a modern, total war and the industrial output of the United States was the hinge on which the outcome of that war turned. The war materiel forged in the "arsenal of democracy" equipped not only the fifteen million Americans mustered into the armed services but, to a considerable extent, the forces of the nation's allies, as well. The Roosevelt administration had sought an antidote for the nation's economic malaise for two full terms. War production was that antidote. The gross national product rose from $91 billion in 1940 to $166 billion in 1945. This explosion was fueled by enormous increases in annual government spending—from $9 billion in 1939 to $100 billion by war's end. The cornucopia of war implements produced included 6,500 warships, 5,400 merchant ships, 296,000 planes, 86,000 tanks, 15,000,000 small arms, 40 billion bullets and 4,000,000 tons of artillery shells at a cost of $186 billion.[1]

The unnatural partnership between the Roosevelt administration and big business, so necessary to the realization of these production miracles, was often stormy, particularly in the time period between the fall of France and Pearl Harbor. The resurgent economy had spurred consumer demand to levels not seen since the 1920s, and American businessmen were in no hurry to convert their factories to the production of tanks and machine guns while there was money to be made selling automobiles and washing machines. As

9

late as January 1942, Detroit was still producing passenger cars. While big business was slow to convert to wartime production, it was also reluctant to reconvert after the production goals had been realized. Leaders of some of the largest companies involved in war production feared that a gradual reconversion, as favored by War Production Board chairman Donald Nelson, would result in small companies gaining an unfair advantage in the postwar marketplace.[2]

A cursory review of the list of war materiel completed should make readily apparent the significance of steel production to the American war effort. The nation's steel industry had reached its productive peak in 1929 with the completion of some sixty-three million net tons, but demand evaporated with the coming of the Depression. By 1932, the industry was functioning at less than 20 percent of capacity; and while the remaining years of the decade showed sporadic improvement, the production total for 1938 was still less than half that achieved before the Depression. Industry capacity in 1940 was 81.6 million net tons, a figure that would prove wholly inadequate to meet the coming demand; but both government and industry were slow to recognize the shortfall. It was not until September 1941 that the Supply, Priorities, and Allocations Board (SPAB) approved a 10 million ton steel expansion program. By 1945, capital expenditures by both the federal government and private industry had resulted in a 18.8 percent increase in total capacity to 96 million tons. By comparison, the total steel production capability of the Axis, including the captive nations of Western Europe, never exceeded 75 million tons.[3]

The three essential commodities necessary to produce steel are coal, limestone, and iron ore. During World War II, the appropriate ratio of these substances required that the domestic mining industry of the nation produce 1.28 tons of coal, .39 tons of limestone and 1.74 tons of iron ore for each ton of pig iron manufactured. Fortunately, the United States had always been self-sufficient in the production of iron ore, mostly due to the vast deposits located in northern Minnesota and the upper peninsula of Michigan. These areas accounted for more than 90 percent of all the iron ore utilized by the United States steel industry during the war. The task of moving the ore from the mines of the frozen north, down the Great Lakes to the steel furnaces of Pittsburgh, Gary, Youngstown, and Detroit was in the hands of twenty companies operating some three hundred bulk freighters in the Great Lakes shipping industry.[4]

The economic vitality of bulk commerce on the Great Lakes has, for generations, been directly tied to the fluctuations of the steel industry, the principal customers for iron ore. As a result, the industry suffered through difficult times throughout the 1930s. Iron ore shipments had plunged from an all-time high of 65.2 million gross tons in 1929 to only 3.5 million gross tons in 1932. This last figure was the smallest amount of ore shipped since the 1880s when the industry was in its infancy. The Lake Carrier's Association reported that only 227 of 405 bulk carriers on the lakes ever left port during the season, many of these making only one or two trips before being laid up again, while the giant Pittsburgh fleet did not fit out its first ship of the season until the second week of June. The season iron ore total represented one-third of the amount moved by the fleet in the single month of August 1929. In addition to the virtual disappearance of iron ore cargos, the movement of soft coal was the lowest since 1924, and grain shipments the lowest since 1920, while anthracite coal totals were the worst since the association had begun keeping records.[5]

Under these circumstances, the shipping companies sought to provide employment for their most experienced people first, with the strange result that ships left port with crews consisting entirely of licensed officers—captains sailing as mates and wheelsmen and mates working as watchmen and even deckhands. Those employed in the unlicensed positions suffered the further indignity of an industry-wide across-the-board pay cut of 20 percent, but most were simply thankful to be working at all.[6]

During the balance of the decade, iron ore demand gradually recovered, reaching a peak of 62.6 million gross tons in 1937 only to plummet again to 19.2 million gross tons the following year. Capital investment was small, since only four new freighters were added to the aging fleet after 1929; and large numbers of the ships were "mothballed" for lack of cargos. The decade-long economic drought had a corresponding effect on shipbuilders around the region, since the lack of new construction and repair contracts forced many small companies to close down or sell out to larger concerns.[7]

In direct contrast to the Depression decade, the years from 1939 to 1945 would see Great Lakes shippers struggling to meet an unprecedented demand for iron ore that would reach a level half again as great as that shipped during the record-breaking 1929 season. Simultaneously, the industry would have to deliver unheard-of quantities of grain, coal, and limestone while competing with the military and industrial employers for scarce workers and resources.

The present study is an effort to tell the story of how those companies working in the water-related industries of the Great Lakes were able to meet the enormous demands placed upon them at a time when failure would have had disastrous consequences for the nation's war effort. Francis Walton referred to the extraordinary American industrial output as "the miracle of World War II." We will look at some of the contributions of the people of the Great Lakes region to the achievement of that "miracle."

11

1
The Great Lakes on the Eve of War

America's five Great Lakes and their tributaries, fresh water all, offer
as thrilling tales of the ships that ply their waters as were ever written
of the seas. Hard, sturdy men have sailed forth upon these lakes in
many types of ships. Indians and early explorers used frail canoes,
much the same as their distant native brothers did along the sea
coasts. Ships on the lakes have developed and improved until today
the modern Great Lakes freighter has no equal for tonnage and
efficiency anywhere in the world.
— Dana Thomas Bowen, 1940

During the peace talks that led to the Treaty of Paris in 1783, the issues of
the northern and western boundaries of the new nation were matters of
intense negotiation. John Adams, serving as plenipotentiary for Congress to secure a peace treaty, had been instructed to insist upon the Mississippi River as the western boundary, while the northwestern line was to extend from the southern end of Lake Nipissing straight to the source of the
Mississippi, which at that time was unknown. These boundaries were wholly
unacceptable to the British, because they would have denied that nation access to the Great Lakes for trading purposes; and Adams's instructions were
subsequently modified to give him greater flexibility in reaching an agreement. The eventual treaty language described the now-familiar rivers and
lakes line from the St. Lawrence, through the Great Lakes, to the Lake of the
Woods. One serendipitous result of the decision to abandon the Lake Nipissing line was the inclusion within the new nation's borders of northeastern
Minnesota's Mesabi and Cuyuna iron ore ranges, the sites of some of the
richest ore deposits on earth. The nation's good fortune continued when the
Webster–Ashburton Treaty of 1842 gave the United States the rest of the
"Arrow Head" region of northeastern Minnesota, which included the Vermilion iron ore range. It appears that neither Daniel Webster nor Great Brit-
ain's Lord Ashburton were aware of the area's great mineral wealth at the
time of the conclusion of the treaty.[1]

13

The first discovery of the rich mineral in the Lake Superior region was probably made by William A. Burt, a government surveyor, who reported in 1845 that the iron ore deposits were disrupting his compass in Michigan's upper peninsula. By 1852, the Cleveland Iron Mining Company was shipping the ore down the lakes to Ohio and Pennsylvania. The process was laborious, since the cargo had to be transferred off of the vessels to wagons in order to circumvent the rapids on the St. Marys River, connecting Lakes Superior and Huron. In 1853, the total shipped amounted to one thousand tons. Additional discoveries led to the identification of six major iron ore ranges: Mesabi, Vermilion, and Cuyuna in Minnesota and Gogebic, Marquette, and Menominee in Michigan. During the last half of the nineteenth century, development of these vast ore fields contributed to the explosive growth of the Great Lakes region into the greatest manufacturing area on earth. The ore was shipped down the lakes to meet with Appalachian coal in the rapidly expanding steel furnaces of Pittsburgh, Youngstown, Gary and Detroit. The bottleneck at the St. Marys Falls was first removed with the installation of a lock to lower vessels from Lake Superior to Lake Huron in 1855, with several additional locks being added over the years.[2]

By the eve of World War II, an extraordinarily complex industry had emerged to move the red mineral from mine to furnace. The ore was removed from open-pit or shaft mines and loaded aboard hopper-bottom railroad cars for transfer to the loading docks at Duluth and Two Harbors, Minnesota; Superior and Ashland, Wisconsin; and Marquette and Escanaba, Michigan. While the cars were en route, chemists would analyze samples of the ore to determine the grade and telephone results ahead to assembly yards at the docks. Here the trains were disassembled and rearranged so that comparable grades of ore could be shipped together. The trains were then driven out onto the massive loading docks, wooden structures 80 feet high, 60 feet wide, and up to 2,300 feet long. The ore was released through the bottom of the cars into pockets in the dock and then loaded into the ships by gravity through long steel chutes. The ships often had to be moved back and forth along the dock to line up with particular pockets and to ensure that the cargo was balanced in the hold of the vessel.[3]

The Great Lakes bulk carrier that had developed over decades of experience was a unique design, with both a forecastle and an after deckhouse. The central portion of the ship had a series of hatches that were removed to allow access to the cargo hold while the propulsion machinery was contained in a separate watertight compartment at the rear. The largest American-flag steamer in use in 1939 was the 631 foot *Harry Coulby* of the Interlake Steamship Company of Cleveland. This ship was 65 feet wide and 33 feet deep and could carry 14,000 tons of ore in a single trip. Most of the larger ships utilized in the ore trade had been built during the 1920s; but some of the smaller, less efficient boats had been around since the turn of the century. The lake freighters spent their entire careers on fresh water avoiding the ravaging effect of salt on their hulls and, as a result, achieved longevity unequaled by ocean vessels. Thus, a steamer such as the *Yosemite*, built in 1901, was still capable of delivering 5,800 tons of ore per trip when the demands of the economy justified its use. The average trip capacity of the 308 American bulk freighters capable of operating in the iron ore trade in 1938 was 8,572 tons.[4]

The crew of a typical Great Lakes bulk carrier consisted of thirty-five to forty men who were divided into very separate and distinct hierarchies on the "forward" and "aft" ends of the boat. The captain was a veteran of the lakes who had risen through the ranks of the company for many years before being assigned the ultimate responsibility of vessel command. Next in rank on the forward end were the first, second, and third mates, who were licensed Great Lakes pilots. By 1939, the crews worked shifts of four hours on and eight hours off, so each mate was actually in charge of the vessel during his shift or "watch," subject only to the ultimate authority of the captain. Additional forward crew included three wheelsmen, three watchmen, and three deck watchmen, one from each group serving with a mate to comprise a watch, while three deckhands worked as a crew on maintenance tasks during daylight hours and handled the ship's lines in port. The deck watchmen also worked with the deckhands during their watch but had the additional responsibility of "sounding" the boat by checking the water level in the ballast tanks at six-hour intervals. The watchmen were posted as lookouts on the forecastle deck and also supervised the deck watch and deckhands.

While the forward crew was primarily concerned with navigation, the aft personnel were responsible for operation of the vessel's propulsion equipment. The chief engineer supervised three assistant engineers who, like the mates at the forward end, were responsible for their individual watches. The engine room also employed three oilers, three coal-passers and, in the typical freighter with two Scotch boilers, six firemen. The primary responsibility of the oiler was to keep the engines lubricated while the firemen worked to maintain steam pressure in the boilers and the coal-passers shoveled coal from the bunkers. The engine room of a coal-burning laker was a hot and dirty place with temperatures well in excess of one hundred degrees. In order to keep up the steam pressure, the firemen had periodically to "wing over" the fire, that is, slide the live coals to one side of the furnace with a large metal bar, then draw the still-red-hot ashes from the furnace, where the coal-passer would dowse them with a bucket of water. After all the ashes were pulled, the coal-passer would shovel them into a reservoir, where they would be washed overboard.

The wheelsmen, watchmen, deck watchmen, oilers, and firemen were certificated by the U.S. Coast Guard on the basis of experience and professional skill, and no vessel was allowed to operate unless it carried the correct number of sailors in these rated positions. Additional crew included two cooks and two porters, who prepared and served the meals; sailors were always eager to ship out on a boat that had acquired a reputation as a "good feeder."

Crew members in licensed and rated positions usually spent the entire navigation season aboard the same vessel without vacation or leave, as it was assumed that the sailors would have an opportunity to spend time with their families ashore during the winter months.* Turnover in the unskilled positions was somewhat more frequent, since these jobs were often filled by young, single men. The shipping companies sought to keep some stability by paying year-end bonuses (five dollars per month plus bus fare home) to men who spent the entire season aboard the same vessel, and a crewman who was aboard a ship at year end was often given the option to start the following season aboard the same ship.[5]

During the 1939 season, less than 10 percent of lake sailors were represented by labor unions. The remarkable success of the industry in resisting the organizational efforts of the maritime unions was due, in large measure, to the office of the Lake Carriers Association (LCA). Created in 1892 by a group of Cleveland vessel owners, the LCA was ostensibly formed to function as a centralized lobbying voice for the bulk carriers; but the primary responsibility of the office was to resist the growth of the organized labor movement on the lakes. During the 1908 and 1909 seasons, the LCA took advantage of a sluggish economy to launch an attack on the unions, declaring an open shop and prohibiting union delegates from boarding their ships. At the same time, the LCA introduced its Welfare Plan that set up owner-controlled hiring halls around the lakes and required that all sailors register with the halls before they could be placed on a vessel. The sailors were issued "continuous record discharge books," which were to be deposited with the captain of each ship when the sailor reported and returned when the sailor left the ship, with a written comment from the captain. If the sailor's perfor-

---

*While it is undoubtedly not true that the average Great Lakes sailor had a girl in every port, a story reported in the *Detroit Free Press* on 22 December 1941 may be instructive. It seems that Captain Elias Andreas, a bachelor, provided a $500 bequest in his will to "my girlfriend at the time of my death." A total of twenty-one women from Duluth, Superior, Ashtabula, Ashland, Milwaukee, Chicago, Erie, and Cleveland applied. In a Solomon-like decision, the judge awarded the money to the only applicant who attended the captain's funeral.

mance was unsatisfactory, the book was not returned, and he was effectively barred from further employment. The Welfare Plan also included death benefits for the survivors of seamen who died in the line of duty.[6]

The industry was successful in crushing the unions: memberships plunged from 8,600 in 1908 to 2,400 in 1915. The LCA continued to employ a policy of benevolent paternalism throughout the 1920s and 1930s. Wages were set at a level slightly higher than those paid to unionized ocean sailors on the coasts, and food and living quarters on lake vessels "were the envy of salt-water sailors." While union memberships were exploding in many other industries, the program of the Great Lakes bulk shippers was so successful that only a few of the smaller vessel operators had been forced into collective bargaining agreements by 1939.[7]

Without the constraints of labor agreements, captains and chief engineers were free to do their own hiring, and they usually chose men who had sailed with them in the past or people from their hometowns. Thus, when the *Charles M. Schwab* set sail for the 1937 season under the command of Captain John Lavely of Marine City, more than half the crew, including the chief engineer and three of the other six officers, were from that tiny St. Clair River town. As one old-timer put it, "You couldn't fart in Superior, the whole town would know it before you got home."[8]

A laden vessel departing from one of the five iron ore loading ports on western Lake Superior began a journey of over a thousand miles that could last for a week. The first and longest leg was across the open waters of Lake Superior in an easterly direction, 383 miles to Sault Ste. Marie. Here the ship would negotiate the famous Soo Locks and pass through the seventy-mile length of the St. Marys River. Upon reaching open water at the head of Lake Huron, about 20 percent of the ships would head west, through the Straits of Mackinac and up the full length of Lake Michigan to the unloading facilities in South Chicago or Gary, Indiana.* The majority of the boats would travel south down Lake Huron and through the St. Clair River, Lake St. Clair and the Detroit River to Lake Erie. These ships would unload their cargos at a dozen separate ports ranging from Detroit in the west to Tonawanda, New York at the extreme eastern end of Lake Erie. The loading port of Escanaba is located on the southern shore of Michigan's Upper Peninsula, at the top of Lake Michigan; thus a ship departing from this port avoided the long trip across Lake Superior and down the St. Marys River. The port of Escanaba was, however, too far away from the bulk of the ore mined in Minnesota;

---

*A "downbound" ship is moving with the current while an "upbound" vessel is traveling against the current. These terms can be confusing when used with regard to Lake Michigan, where the water flows in a northerly direction.

and it was more economical to ship the commodity by vessel from Duluth and Superior than to haul it to Escanaba by rail. As a result, only about 7 percent of the total iron ore production was shipped from Escanaba.[9]

Upon its arrival at one of the principal unloading ports, the lake freighter would be relieved of its cargo with a device known as a Hulett unloader. This machine featured an enormous set of jaws, capable of holding eighteen tons of ore in a single bite; the operator actually rode the device down into the hold of the ship, sitting in a small compartment in the shaft. The long arm of the crane was mounted on a chassis that rode along railroad tracks parallel to the dock. Utilizing the Hulett, bulk freighters were unloaded in an average time of five to six hours. After unloading, the iron ore was stockpiled for later shipment by train to the steel mills.[10]

In addition to iron ore, Great Lakes vessels engaged in delivering three other important bulk cargos: coal, grain, and limestone. Prior to World War II, the coal trade on the Great Lakes involved a movement of that commodity that was virtually the opposite of that for iron ore. Most of the bituminous coal burned in the homes and factories of the Midwest was mined in Appalachia and much of it was shipped up the Great Lakes after being carried by rail to one of ten Lake Erie ports. It was a common practice for freighters to pick up a load of coal after discharging a load of iron ore. This would allow the vessel owners more economical operation, since the ship would not have to return back up the lakes without a cargo. Much of the grain shipped on the lakes originated in the Lake Superior ports of Thunder Bay, Ontario, and Duluth as harvests from the great agricultural heartland of North America were sent to these cities by rail for movement down the lakes and on to the population centers of the east and to eastern seaports for shipment abroad. Movement of much of this bulk commodity had traditionally been done by the Canadian fleet, but American bulk carriers had played a significant role, particularly in the fall of the year when competitive pricing to move the harvest could be more profitable to a vessel operator than ore shipments.[11]

The last bulk cargo handled in significant quantities by the Great Lakes shipping industry was limestone, which is also used in the production of steel. Much of the limestone was mined in the Alpena area of Michigan's Lower Peninsula and shipped to the industrial centers. Because cargos of stone and coal often had to be discharged at docks that did not have sophisticated unloading equipment, the industry had developed self-unloading vessels for use in these trades. These ships were equipped with conveyer belts that ran beneath the cargo holds and were capable of off-loading the substance by use of these belts and long booms that could be swung over the ship's side. During the postwar era, the self-unloader would evolve into the standard lake vessel configuration; but in 1938 there were only fifty-four ships so equipped in the American fleet.[12]

One dominant, limiting factor that has always affected the ability of the Great Lakes shipping industry to deliver its cargos has been the weather. All six of the major ranges were north of the forty-fifth parallel, and the harsh weather rendered shipments virtually impossible after winter's onset. Fierce storms swept the lakes during November, but the ships traditionally operated until 1 December, after which time the dangers occasioned by ice conditions made insurance unavailable. The shipping ports on western Lake Superior would remain choked with ice until some time in April or May, and the narrow channels of the St. Marys, St. Clair, and Detroit Rivers were also impassable. Low temperatures on the ranges would cause the moisture in the ore to freeze, necessitating the difficult and time-consuming process of "steaming" the ore before it could be transferred from the trains to the boats.* Of course, conditions would vary, depending on the severity of the winter weather, but the shipping season would generally run from the middle of April to 1 December. This limiting factor required that the carriers deliver and stockpile at the unloading ports a sufficient quantity of iron ore to satisfy the demands of their customers throughout the winter season. Ground storage capacity at the unloading ports totaled about thirty million tons, a capacity that had been sufficient to meet the steel industry demand during the winter. With the coming of spring, the ore boats would rush back into operation to replenish the dwindled supply.[13]

During the 1920s, as many as 350 companies were operating ships in Great Lakes commerce, but this number plunged rapidly during the Depression, as marginal operations folded. Many smaller companies were not able to raise sufficient capital to invest in the larger steel freighters required to operate competitively in the iron ore trade, and the trend was toward the concentration of carrying capacity in a handful of larger corporations. By 1938, twenty-one United States companies were operating 308 vessels in the Great Lakes ore trade. These firms ranged in size from the industry giant, Pittsburgh Steamship Company, with seventy-nine boats, down to several lines operating as few as two vessels each. Several of the larger carriers were actually wholly owned subsidiaries of major iron ore producers. The best example of this vertical integration of the ore industry was the U.S. Steel Company, which owned controlling interests in the great Mesabi Range, the

---

*The steam was generated by a locomotive engine and run through hoses to metal probes which were inserted in ports built into the sides of the railroad hopper cars. The heat would then rise through the ore, melting the frozen moisture, and the car was quickly run up onto the dock and dumped before the water could refreeze.

railroads that linked the range with the ore docks, and the Pittsburgh fleet that transported the ore to the company's mills. Other ore producers with in-house fleets included Pickands, Mather and Company (Interlake Steamship Company), Cleveland–Cliffs Iron Company (Cleveland–Cliffs Steamship Company) and Oglebay, Norton and Company (Columbia Transportation Company). Virtually all of the major companies involved in the shipment of bulk commodities were members of the LCA, and each was assessed fees to support this organization that were based on the number of vessels operating in their fleet. During the war years, this office would develop into the principal voice representing the industry in dealing with the federal government.[14]

While the Great Lakes shipping industry of the prewar era was dominated by the bulk carriers, hundreds of sailors also made a living manning passenger ships, package freighters, tankers, and car ferries. During the nineteenth century, passenger ships had played a major role in the explosive growth and development of Buffalo, Cleveland, Detroit, Chicago, and Milwaukee by transporting thousands of immigrants from the east; and for generations thereafter, these ships provided fast and economical transportation between these major cities and scores of lesser ports around the lakes. The phenomenal rise of the automobile in the 1920s presaged the decline of passenger ships as a competitive means of transportation; and by 1939, only a handful of companies still offered such service. Most notable among these were the Cleveland and Buffalo Steamship Company, the Detroit and Cleveland Navigation Company and the Chicago, Duluth and Georgian Bay Transit Company. These fleets operated large, palatial steamers such as the *Seeandbee* and the *City of Detroit III* on regular routes between major ports and advertised vacation cruises around the lakes.

Competition from the rapidly developing trucking industry had an even more devastating effect on the fleets engaged in the package trade on the lakes. The largest of these, the Great Lakes Transit Corporation, had suffered financial losses in every season since 1933, while its chief competitor, the Minnesota–Atlantic Transit Company had not shown a profit since 1923. As a result, only sixteen ships were still operated in this trade at the beginning of the war.[15]

In addition to the economic paralysis of the Great Depression, shipbuilding on the Great Lakes at the close of the decade was constrained by two overriding considerations, one political and the other geographical. The Rush–Bagot Agreement of 1817 prohibited the construction of warships on the Great Lakes, with the result that Great Lakes yards had no significant history of successful completion of government construction projects prior to World War I. During 1917–18, the provisions of the treaty were suspended by mutual agreement with Canada; and the Great Lakes builders did complete numerous small craft for military use. However, the suspension was terminated at the close of hostilities, and the treaty remained in effect as World War II approached. The geographical constraint was one that could not be "suspended" by mutual consent: the canals around the Lachine, Soulanges, and International Rapids on the St. Lawrence River limited passage to vessels with a maximum length of 259 feet and a maximum draft of 14 feet. As a result of these factors, new construction on the Great Lakes had traditionally been limited almost exclusively to vessels designed solely for use on the lakes. During the decade of the 1930s, there had been precious little new construction; even repair-and-maintenance contracts were greatly curtailed, causing many of the smaller shipyards to close down or sell out to larger concerns.[16]

2
1939-1941: The Coming Storm

What you see here is a selective look at what was once the present—
what I have called "the borrowed years," when most of my friends and
I were singing and dancing and laughing away the last hours of youth
while the lights, as they used to say, were going out all over the world.
　　　　　　　　　　　　　　　　　　—Richard M. Ketchum

In 1941 the world lived on the edge of hell.

　　　　　　　　　　　　　　　　　　—William K. Klingaman

O n 28 April 1939, the steamer *Philip D. Block* passed upbound through
the Soo Locks and into Lake Superior, inaugurating the final season of a
decade that most Great Lakes iron ore shippers were quite willing to forget. The Great Depression had idled hundreds of vessels and sent thousands
of sailors looking for scarce jobs ashore. The brief recovery of 1937 had
fizzled, unemployment was again on the rise, and there was no indication
that the nation would again see a healthy economy anytime soon. From our
vantage point, it is difficult to appreciate the pessimism and despair engen-
dered by a solid decade of depression. When twenty-year-old Robert Burns
landed a job as a fireman on the *Fayette Brown*, the engineer told him,
"There's the coal pile, there's the shovel, there's the steam gauge, if you can't
keep the steam up there's two hundred men ashore waitin' for your job!"—a
remark that in many ways typified attitudes on the eve of the war years.[1]

During the 1938 season, the boats had moved only 19,263,011 tons of
iron ore, the lowest total, with the exception of the disastrous 1932 season,
since the Lake Carriers Association had begun to keep records. Some opti-
mistic observers of the ore trade predicted that demand would be double
that of the previous year; but even that rate would leave the industry functioning at a level far below capacity, while a strike in the bituminous coal
fields promised a paucity of cargos in even the most stable of the bulk commodities.[2]

23

In Europe, the democracies had postponed the outbreak of war in the fall of 1938 with the shameful bargain at Munich, but the United States had failed to take advantage of the delay to upgrade its woeful military establishment, which *Life* referred to as "the smallest, worst-equipped armed force of any major power." President Franklin D. Roosevelt recognized the danger that European war posed to his country, but he faced powerful isolationist and noninterventionist blocs in Congress, as well as public opinion solidly opposed to American involvement in European disputes. The Neutrality Acts of 1935, 1936, and 1937 prohibited both the carrying of arms to belligerents in American vessels and the granting of loans to nations at war, while the parsimonious Congress refused to allocate funds for increasing American military preparedness. As a result, the heavy industrial segments of the economy were relying solely on the weak domestic markets for orders well into the summer of 1939. Iron ore movement accurately reflected the state of the economy through the end of August as shippers utilized only 60 percent of their vessels to deliver 22,501,290 gross tons,* a figure less than half of that totaled during the comparable period in the recovery year of 1937.[3]

Hitler's invasion of Poland on 1 September gave an immediate jolt to the long-slumbering American economy as millions of consumers cleared store shelves in a flurry of spending and hoarding; the nation's gross national product increased in the last quarter at a rate of twice that shown in the first nine months of 1939. Even though no large orders for munitions had yet been received, manufacturers sought to stockpile material for future use, and automotive manufacturers raised production goals for 1940 from three to four million units. These developments were immediately felt on the lakes as steel concerns sought to replenish ore supplies before winter's onset. During September, October, and November, the industry moved 22,506,318 gross tons of ore, an amount that had not been seen in a corresponding period since 1926.[4]

To meet this sudden and unanticipated demand, shippers fitted out and placed in service dozens of boats during the months of September and October, a time that normally found the industry laying up vessels for the winter. Between 15 August and 23 September, at least forty-six additional freighters joined the ore fleet, and fourteen of the twenty-one companies operating in the trade reported all of their ships in operation. The weatherman also cooperated as summerlike conditions prevailed on the upper lakes well into December, so that when the steamer *Captain C. D. Secord* locked down

---

*A gross (or long) ton contains 2,240 pounds, while a net (or short) ton contains 2,000 pounds. The Great Lakes shipping industry reported iron ore totals in gross tons, while other bulk commodities were reported in net tons.

through the Soo on 14 December, closing the season, the St. Marys River was still ice-free.[5]

Following the German Wehrmacht's blitzkrieg of Poland, the situation in Europe stabilized into the "phony war" that lasted throughout the winter of 1939-40. England and France seemed strangely reluctant to come to grips with the task ahead, and the world buzzed with rumors of a negotiated peace. In the United States, the economy slowed once again; it appeared that the boom had quickly run its course. But with the coming of spring, Hitler unleashed his forces in the west, overrunning Denmark, Norway, and the Netherlands in a matter of days and then plunging into France. A stunned America watched in awe as the proud French army, which had held the Germans on the Western Front for four terrible years in the Great War, was shattered in just six weeks.

The reality of the war in Europe was brought closer to home by the plight of ships and crews orphaned on the Great Lakes by the Nazi juggernaut. By 1939, vessels from Norway, Finland, and the Netherlands, being small enough to transit the St. Lawrence Canal, were making regular calls at Great Lakes ports. These ships would deliver cargos of newsprint, codliver oil, and canned fish and would return to Europe with automobiles, pig iron, structural steel, or even wheat from as far inland as Duluth. In September of that year, fourteen crew members of the Finnish ship *Maud Thoren* refused to leave the dock in Detroit to pick up a load of pig iron bound for Gothenburg, Sweden. The crew reportedly feared the presence of mines in the Baltic and were unwilling to ship out, even when offered higher wages. The matter was resolved after several days, when the men were paid off and a new crew of American and Canadian able-bodied seamen was recruited.[6]

Incidents of this type became far more complex after Hitler's lightning conquests of the following spring. Queen Wilhelmina of the Netherlands and King Haakon VII of Norway both fled to London, where their respective governments in exile instructed all of their merchant sailors to submit to British authority for the rest of the war. Several vessels on the Great Lakes were directly affected by these tumultuous events, and newspapers around the lakes reported the stories of sailors who had left port with their country at peace only now to face an uncertain and dangerous future without word or contact from loved ones left behind on the Nazi-occupied continent. By far the most dramatic of these incidents involved the strange saga of the Dutch freighter *Prins Willem II*, a story that read like a spy novel to those throughout the Midwest who closely followed newspaper accounts during the summer months of 1940.[7]

The 260-foot Oranje Line vessel was docked in Chicago in mid-May when word was received of the fall of the Netherlands. As a result of a presidential proclamation freezing assets of invaded nations, no funds were available to pay the crew; yet according to the Dutch consul, crew members returned from a shore leave "intoxicated" and with "plenty of money." They had apparently paid a visit to the German consul in Chicago, where they had been encouraged to resist delivering their ship to a British port. On 8 June, the ship sailed to Sandusky, Ohio and was loaded with a cargo of coal for Montreal, but the crew informed Captain P. G. W. C. van der Eyck that they would not sail to that Canadian port. Two members of the crew left the ship in Sandusky and attempted to hitchhike back to Chicago, but these individuals were apprehended by immigration officials and returned to the ship. For several weeks, Captain Eyck and Dutch consular officials negotiated with the recalcitrant crew, attempting to convince them to honor Queen Wilhelmina's proclamation; but on 5 July, Dutch authorities, reporting threats of sabotage from the crew, declared them guilty of "mutiny, desertion, disloyalty and treason," and the U.S. Coast Guard was ordered to seize the vessel. Twenty members of the crew, including chief engineer Franz Heydens, who was described as their leader, were held in Sandusky's Erie County Jail while federal immigration officials debated their status. A subsequent search of the vessel revealed no sabotage, and on 11 July, eight of the crew, including Heydens and six other officers, were released after they agreed to resume their duties aboard the ship. The remaining twelve sailors were transferred to Detroit for deportation hearings.[8]

While the events of 11 July broke the Sandusky stalemate, it was not the end of the strange odyssey of the *Prins Willem II*. After departing port with a dozen new Canadian crew members, Captain Eyck received another rude surprise when he attempted to guide his ship into the Welland Canal at Port Colborne, Ontario. Apparently unconvinced of the sincerity of Engineer Heyden's abnegation, Canadian officials ordered the ship to the wall, where a squad of twelve mounties boarded her and conducted a thorough search. Heydens was arrested and shipped to a Canadian prison camp. Six of the twelve sailors held in Detroit subsequently agreed to serve aboard a Dutch merchantman and were transferred to New York and placed aboard a ship; the remaining six were convicted as undesirable aliens and ordered deported, but they remained interned in Detroit, since no means existed of carrying out the deportation order. In one final ironic twist, these six celebrated their good fortune the following spring when newspapers reported the loss of the *Prins Willem II* to a German torpedo attack in the North Atlantic. Eight of her crew were rescued from an open life boat, but Captain Eyck apparently went down with his ship.[9]

From the opening of hostilities, the German U-boat campaign in the Atlantic destroyed hundreds of thousands of tons of commercial shipping creating a worldwide demand for replacement tonnage. Great Lakes package freighters and canal-sized ships were a logical source, and among the first to go were the vessels of the Minnesota–Atlantic Company, better known around the lakes as the "Poker Fleet." These boats had originally been constructed for the U.S. Shipping Board in Great Lakes yards during World War I, but the war was over by the time they were launched, and they remained on the lakes. In 1924, the Minnesota–Atlantic Transit Company purchased five of these surplus vessels and renamed them *Ace, King, Queen, Jack, and Ten*—hence the "Poker Fleet."* Since these ships were originally designed for ocean duty, they were small enough to transit the St. Lawrence canals and they were equipped with surface condensers to reuse fresh water, thus making them relatively simple to reconvert for saltwater use. In 1940, the *Queen* and the *Ten* were sold to the government of Brazil, while the other three boats followed their sisters to salt water the following year, when they were sold to the U.S. Maritime Commission.

The blitz of France and the Low Countries had a galvanizing effect upon the American public, and Roosevelt was finally able to garner support for rearming the nation. In an address to a joint session of Congress, the president called for the production of fifty thousand airplanes; Congress responded by appropriating billions of dollars for defense expenditures. To oversee his defense program, Roosevelt created the National Defense Advisory Commission (NDAC) in June, 1940. This board consisted of a group of experts in the areas of production, transportation, and farming; but, characteristically, Roosevelt kept control in his own hands by failing to give the new group specific direction or powers. Roosevelt appointed Ralph Budd as transportation commissioner, a sixty-year-old railroad executive, who quickly recruited LCA president Alexander T. Wood, the "tall, dapper," thirty-eight-year-old Harvard Master of Business Administration, as his expert on Great Lakes shipping problems. As the NADC's title suggests, the agency functioned in a purely advisory capacity, exercising no direct authority over the shipping industry.[10]

Ore shipments started slowly during the 1940 season, since ice conditions delayed the first cargo from Escanaba until 20 April and many ore carriers were utilized in the coal trade until the early summer. In addition to difficulties with ice, sailors encountered storm warnings on the lakes four times during the last two weeks of April; one of these blows caused the loss of the Canadian steamer *Arlington*. The 259-foot grain ship had left Fort William on the evening of 30 April with a cargo of wheat accompanied by

---

*The Minnesota–Atlantic Transit Co. also owned the *Nine*, a smaller and older ship that was sold for scrap in 1941.

the larger Canada Steamship Lines vessel *Collingwood*. The weather worsened during the night, and the smaller ship began to take on water, so that by dawn, Captain Fred Burke realized that his ship was foundering and ordered his crew to take to the lifeboats. In order to safely launch the small boats on the wild lake, Captain Burke stayed at the wheel of his vessel to steady its course until his sixteen-man crew was clear. Shortly thereafter, the *Arlington* plunged to the bottom, taking her master with her, while the rest of the crew were rescued by the *Collingwood*. The loss of the *Arlington* and her brave skipper was a mere preamble to what the balance of the 1940 season would bring.[11]

After the fall of France, iron-ore demand expanded quickly. The *Cleveland Plain Dealer* reported that 291 of 297 bulk carriers were active in the ore trade by 15 June, up from 218 a month earlier. By 15 September, the same paper was reporting that the industry was operating at 100 percent capacity for the first time since August of 1937.[12]

The fall of the year brought miserable weather with dense fog and heavy gales, causing the LCA to lament: "Almost invariably late navigation has been characterized by summer sailing schedules in lean seasons of freight demand and by unfavorable weather in seasons when there was urgent need for unhampered vessel operations until the end of November. From a navigational point of view the fall of 1940 was one of the worst in a decade."[13] Of particularly deadly effect was the famous Armistice Day Storm of 11 November, which concentrated its wrath on Lake Michigan. This storm is generally considered to be second only to the Great Storm of 1913 in power and destructive force. The vicious cyclone packed sustained southwest winds of fifty miles per hour, with gusts as high as eighty, a force powerful enough to drop the water level at Chicago by nearly five feet, with a corresponding increase in the water levels at the northern end of the lake. At Houghton, Michigan, the barometric pressure dropped to 996 millibars (28.57 inches of mercury) one of the lowest pressures ever recorded in the Great Lakes region. The wind caused extensive damage throughout the Midwest, with the states of Illinois, Minnesota, and Michigan being hardest hit, fifty-six deaths being attributed to the storm. Transportation and communication facilities were crippled throughout the region, including the destruction of the 733-foot broadcast tower of Detroit's WJR radio station.[14]

Given the extent of damage ashore, it is not difficult to imagine the deadly consequences of the blow on the open waters of the Great Lakes—an entire generation of retired lake sailors looks back upon the storm as the worst in their experience. During the early morning hours of Monday, 11 November, the storm approached Lake Michigan with strong southeast winds; and the freighter traffic moved along the eastern shore of the lake, where the Michigan shoreline offered relative protection. Before noon, however, a cold front associated with the storm swept across the lake and the winds turned to the southwest and intensified rapidly. This wind shift caught the majority of Lake Michigan traffic along the now-exposed Michigan coastline, and the powerful winds soon built mountainous waves along the full north–south fetch of the lake. Soon the crews of dozens of ships were fighting for their lives on the wildest day ever seen on Lake Michigan.

Aboard Nicholson Transit's 247-foot crane ship *Tampico*, bleary-eyed third mate John LeCorn took over the watch at midnight on the eleventh as his little ship moved southbound on Lake Michigan near the port of Manistee. Fifteen minutes into his watch, he checked the ship's barometer and was surprised to see a reading much lower than that reported to him by the second mate at the time of his relief. After another fifteen-minute interval, the next check of the instrument revealed that the second mate had not made a mistake, since the glass had dropped an equal amount in that short time period. LeCorn immediately awoke the captain, and the decision was made to seek safe harbor for the heavily laden little vessel. When LeCorn returned to the pilot house, he observed the lights of another ship following close behind the *Tampico* on the still quiet water, so he circled out into the lake and around behind the other vessel as he headed for the shelter of Manistee. As he passed under the stern of the ship he could clearly observe the name *William B. Davock*. LeCorn was probably the last person to see this ship afloat.[15]

The storm broke some twelve hours after the *Tampico* was safely tied up in Manistee harbor; and LeCorn retired to his room and his powerful hallocrafter radio for an experience "you just couldn't believe," listening to the ships still out on the lake struggling to stay afloat and off the beach. The *Thomas F. Cole* and a Socony oil tanker were in trouble at the southern end of the lake with damage to their rudders and steering gear, while the pilot-house windows were blown in on the *Frank Billings* and the observation room blasted to "kindling" on *The Harvester*. Over all the other radio noise could be heard distress calls from the captain of the steamer *Frank J. Peterson*, who finally reported his ship hard aground on Hog Island. The next morning, LeCorn heard the skipper of a passing ship politely inform the captain that he was not on Hog Island at all but, in fact, on St. Helena Island, some twenty-five miles to the northeast! When the storm-tossed waters of the northern lake receded, the ship was so hard aground that she was abandoned by her owners as a constructive total loss and was not salvaged until the following spring.[16]

One of the wildest rides of all on that fateful day was experienced by Edward Baganz and the crew of the 549-foot *George W. Perkins* of the Pittsburgh Steamship Company. The colorful Baganz began his career on the Great Lakes when he was literally shanghaied as a dishwasher aboard the sidewheeler *Owana* at the age of fourteen. Despite only an eighth-grade education, he rose to be commodore of the Pittsburgh fleet by the time of his retirement in 1967. The 1940 season was his first as a captain; and late in the year, he was assigned to the *Perkins* in temporary relief of her regular skipper.[17]

On Armistice Day, Baganz brought his ship through Grays Reef Passage and down the Michigan shoreline bound for Chicago with a load of ore. By 4:00 P.M., the ship was off Point Betsie Light near Frankfort, Michigan, sheltered from the southeast winds, when Baganz picked up a Coast Guard weather report advising of "southwest to northwest winds, whole gale." Recognizing that this wind shift would leave him in a perilous position, he immediately turned his ship due west, heading straight across the lake, hoping to find calmer seas along the Wisconsin shore as the wind turned from the southwest to northwest. For several hours, the ship held a steady course bearing on the opening of the Sturgeon Bay Canal, while the winds turned to the southwest, building enormous waves over the three-hundred-mile expanse of open water. After approaching as near as possible to the Wisconsin shore, Baganz again turned his ship to the south but the boat made little progress against the combination of wind and water. As each huge wave rolled under the ship, lifting the stern, the propeller would rise completely out of the water, spinning free. In order to avoid damage to it, the engineer would "check down" the engine with a hand throttle each time the stern went up into the air.

After just a few minutes on the southerly track the wheelsman hollered to Baganz that he could no longer hold the course since the gale was forcing the bow of the ship around, threatening to slide the vessel into the trough of the big waves. Baganz quickly signaled the engine room for full power and successfully turned his boat completely around, now heading north, running with the wind and seas. As darkness fell over Lake Michigan, the winds were blowing at a constant seventy-five to eighty miles per hour, and the waves were estimated to be fifty feet high. Baganz hoped to find shelter in Green Bay, but the narrow Rock Island Passage was obscured by the swirling snow, and he had no choice but to continue north toward the top of the lake.

Without benefit of loran or radar, Baganz and his crew were navigating by dead reckoning ("by guess and by God!"). They now plotted a course for Lansing Shoal, a lighthouse marking the westernmost approach to the Straits of Mackinac and a point some seventy miles from Rock Island Passage. The difficulties inherent in dead reckoning cannot be overemphasized under the conditions that existed on Lake Michigan that evening: the wind, seas, and constant throttling of the engine made course and speed estimations crude at best. The chances of finding the lighthouse were further reduced when the Coast Guard informed all shipping on the northern lake that the storm had knocked out the main light at Lansing Shoals.

For the next several hours, the *Perkins* churned on to the northeast until the lookouts spotted the Gull Island Light "on the wrong side of the steering pole," the ship having strayed some ten miles to the east of the intended course. With Gull Island as an accurate beginning point, *Baganz* plotted a new course for Lansing Shoal, which was now only eighteen miles away. For the next ninety minutes, the tension built in the crowded pilot house as all eyes strained to spot some sign of the lighthouse through the swirling snow. At Lansing Shoal, the ship would turn directly east and would quickly come under the lee shore of Garden Island, where Baganz hoped to anchor. The danger was that if the ship turned east too soon it would run into the shallow reefs surrounding Garden Island, while if the ship moved past Lansing Shoal, it would soon pile onto the treacherous rocks to the northwest of the lighthouse.

As the minutes passed with no sighting, Baganz was about to attempt to turn the ship around and try to fight back down the lake, when the watchman sighted a cluster of blurry lights through the snow off the starboard bow. At first it appeared that the lights must belong to another steamer, but then the crew realized that the lights were blinking on and off. "That's Lansing Shoals, hard over!" Baganz shouted. The crew of the lighthouse had recognized the lights of the approaching ship and were frantically blinking their house lights on and off in an effort to warn her of her location. As the ship veered sharply to the right, it seemed that the steering pole would clip the lighthouse; but, aided by the backwash from the prop and the unusually high water, the ship slid by without a scratch. Twenty minutes later, the *Perkins* was safely anchored in the lee of Garden Island. Baganz called the ship's escape a "miracle," estimating that another minute on her course would have sent the ship piling on the rocks.

While Lake Michigan spared the crew of the *Perkins*, others were less fortunate. The bulk freighter *William B. Davock* of the Interlake Steamship Company, last seen by John LeCorn in the early morning hours of 11 November, sank near Pentwater, Michigan, with the loss of her entire crew of thirty-two sailors, while the Canadian steamer *Anna C. Minch* was lost in the same area with her crew of twenty-four. The canal-sized freighter *Novadoc* was driven aground off Juniper Beach near Little Sable Point, and the surf broke the ship in half. Two men were washed overboard, but the remaining crew members were rescued by the fishing tug *Three Brothers*. Two other fishing tugs went down near South Haven with the loss of eight more lives.

31

The *City of Flint, Conneaut, Sinaloa,* and *Arthur Orr* were all driven ashore at various points around the lake but later recovered.

In deaths and destruction, the Armistice Day Storm is exceeded only by the Great Storm of 1913—and in the opinion of at least one survivor of both, the 1940 blow was "even more severe than the disastrous storm during the fall of 1913." Those who survived its fury would never forget the experience. As Commodore Baganz recalls: "That was the first time I ever was scart'. I'd been in a lot of storms, they never bothered me but this time I thought this was it."[18]

Despite the problems with Mother Nature, the Great Lakes bulk fleet achieved some imposing statistics during the 1940 season, including the delivery of 63,712,982 gross tons of iron ore, the largest total since 1929 and the third largest in history. Coal shipments were in excess of 49,000,000 net tons, and the total bulk freight of 142,874,985 net tons represented the greatest amount ever transported in a single season.[19]

As impressive as these numbers were, they only served to underscore the difficulties ahead; for it was apparent that the 1941 season was going to require even greater totals—numbers beyond the ability of the industry to deliver with normal methods and practices. This was the concern of Transportation Director Budd when he wrote to President Wood of the LCA in December, requesting suggestions for increasing the ore movement during the next season. In response, Wood listed five alternatives, several of which would represent significant deviations from "business as usual" in the industry. Foremost on Wood's list was the use of Canadian vessels in the ore trade; protectionist federal legislation prohibited the operation of foreign-flag ships between two United States ports, eliminating all Canadian vessels from the American ore movement. Federal legislation would be necessary to create an exception for the Great Lakes if Canadian ships were to be utilized. Wood also recommended deeper loading, increased running speeds, Sunday and holiday unloading, and accelerated dispatch of the ships by means of exchange or trading of cargos. This final suggestion, which had been successfully utilized during World War I, would have LCA representatives functioning as central dispatchers to direct a ship to the next available dock and cargo, without regard to company contractual commitments, thus allowing the entire industry to function as a single unit.[20]

On 29 December 1940, President Roosevelt addressed the nation in one of the most important of his famous "fireside chats," urging his countrymen to greater production efforts: "We must be the great arsenal of democracy. For us this is an emergency as serious as war itself." But while most Americans now recognized the need for arming the nation, considerable disagreement still existed on methods and timing. New Dealers charged industry with refusing to convert to weapons production while profits were available in the booming consumer sector—particularly in the automobile industry, where full production continued throughout 1940. Meanwhile, the surging Organized Labor movement sought to improve its position in the expanding economy, and the nation was rocked with defense strikes. Amid all the finger pointing, one fact was clear: the defense buildup was behind schedule and moving at a snail's pace.[21]

In January 1941, Roosevelt sought to answer his critics with a shakeup of the program, scrapping the NDAC and replacing it with the Office of Production Management (OPM) under the coleadership of General Motors executive William Knudsen and labor leader Sidney Hillman. This "strange creation, which, like the imperial Russian eagle, had two heads facing in opposite directions," was supposed to have greater power and a clearer mandate than its predecessor; but again, Roosevelt had avoided creating ultimate authority in a single production head. Fortunately for the situation on the lakes, Ralph Budd continued in the position of transportation commissioner in the new agency, thus perpetuating the relationship with Wood that would show significant results in the near future.[22]

Another example of the confusion in the defense program involved efforts to project the maximum possible output of the American steel industry, an issue of extreme importance to the Great Lakes shippers charged with supplying sufficient ore to reach that maximum. The efforts to superimpose a defense program atop a fully functioning civilian economy "excited the fears of some steel users and encouraged speculative buying." In a press release on 11 October 1940, the American Iron and Steel Institute denied the existence of any shortage in the steel industry, confidently predicting, "Present producing capacity . . . is ample to meet all essential needs now in sight, and no large scale expansion of basic facilities is needed." President Roosevelt asked former U.S. Steel president Edward Stettinius to investigate the productive capacity of the steel industry, and his subsequent report predicted a ten-million-ton surplus for 1942. Privately, however, considerable doubt existed as to the accuracy of these sanguine predictions. In a letter to Wood dated 5 December 1940, deputy transportation commissioner Karl W. Fischer stated: "There is a division of opinion in the steel industry of the ability to meet the defense demands and still avoid any serious curtailment of ordinary consumer demand. I am of the opinion that . . . the steel industry is incapable of meeting all requirements, especially during the year 1941." In the same letter, Fischer informed Wood of a proposed production expansion of 1.2 million tons by Bethlehem Steel Company that would be completed within six months, thus requiring additional transportation tonnage for the coming season. The steel industry predictions proved erroneous, since the

33

nation faced an eleven-million-ton steel shortfall by the end of 1941, thus necessitating a costly and time-consuming steel expansion program.[23]

Given the difficulties in accurately predicting demand, it was concluded "that the 1941 season will be one in which just about all the ore should be moved that it is practicable to move," with projections that the figure would reach eighty million gross tons—a 22 percent increase over the greatest single-season tonnage ever shipped. With this tremendous movement contemplated, it was fortuitous that the weather cooperated in the spring of 1941, as unseasonably mild temperatures allowed the loading of the first ore cargo at Escanaba on 3 April, the earliest date in history. During the month of April, nearly seven million gross tons of ore were delivered, near double the largest previous total for that month; and the records continued to fall with each month's total through September.[24]

The implementation of several of the suggestions made by Wood in his December letter significantly aided the Great Lakes fleet in increasing its totals. The most important of these was the adoption of a system of centralized dispatching handled by a committee of the LCA, which sought to avoid delays in loading or unloading cargos by routing ships to ports and docks without regard to contracts or shipping lines. During peacetime, a freighter of the Pittsburgh Steamship Company bringing ore down to Lake Erie would unload its cargo at Conneaut, Lorain, or Central Furnace in Cleveland. If these docks were busy, the ship would check down its speed to time its arrival with the departure of the earlier ship or anchor until the dock was available. With centralized dispatching, the boat was just as likely to be sent to Toledo, Buffalo, or Erie, depending on the number of boats ahead of it at each location. This system essentially left the entire industry operating as one fleet for dispatch purposes, and it was effective in lowering the average time spent in port for ships discharging cargo to seven hours and twenty-five minutes, down from the previous record of eight hours and fifty-four minutes. Another recommendation of the LCA that materially aided in lowering time spent in port was the Sunday and holiday operation of the unloading rigs, some of which had remained idle on these days to avoid paying overtime rates to the Hulett operators and other shore personnel.[25]

Wood's proposal to lift the ban on Canadian vessel activity in the ore trade was also adopted. Legislation offered by Michigan senator Prentiss H. Brown temporarily suspending the prohibition on the Great Lakes was passed in May of 1941, but the initial results were disappointing. Canadian shippers had greeted the lifting of the ban with enthusiasm, and it was assumed that their vessels would be able to add at least 2.5 million tons to the season totals; but unexpectedly high demand for Canadian grain cargos in early summer delayed entry of the ships into the ore trade until August, and the season total hauled by Canadian flag steamers was only 712,500 gross tons.[26]

Despite this disappointment, iron ore totals continued at a record pace until October, when a serious accident at the Soo Locks brought all shipments to a temporary halt. On 7 October, a locomotive and tender ran through a stop and plunged through an open, bascule-type railroad bridge, collapsing the arm of the bridge into the narrow canal that served as the approach to the American locks. Two of the shallower locks remained open, allowing unloaded ships to pass upbound into Lake Superior; but these were of insufficient depth to allow passage of loaded ore carriers, over 125 of which were soon at anchor above the locks. Engineers worked feverishly to remove the engine and bridge from the lock approach and traffic was resumed three days later. The LCA estimated that somewhere between five hundred thousand and one million gross tons of ore shipments were lost to the accident; and as a result, October was the only month of the 1941 season in which a new monthly record was not achieved. The Soo accident notwithstanding, the industry was able to attain its preseason goal: 80,116,360 gross tons of iron ore were delivered. In addition, season records were set for coal and limestone shipments—the total net tonnage for all bulk cargos was 169,020,975, an increase of 18.3 percent over the previous year's all-time record.[27]

While Great Lakes shippers were meeting the demands created by the defense buildup, their shipbuilding cousins ashore were also welcoming an unprecedented flood of new military orders. On 9 September 1940, the federal government awarded a contract for the construction of ten submarines to the Manitowoc Shipbuilding Company of Manitowoc, Wisconsin. The sixty-million-dollar contract included an initial payment of one million dollars for plant expansion necessary for submarine construction; and by April of the following year, nearly twelve hundred workers were employed at the shipyard. The vessels to be constructed were full-size fleet submarines with a length of 307 feet, a dimension that prohibited delivery down the St. Lawrence. When completed, the ships would be sent to New Orleans by means of the Chicago Drainage Canal and the Mississippi River. The major drawback to this route was a depth limitation of nine feet, a problem overcome by the construction of special shallow draft transit barges similar to drydocks that held the submarines during the journey.[28]

While the Manitowoc contract was the largest awarded to a Great Lakes shipbuilder during the prewar buildup, numerous other concerns around the lakes were also helping to fill the government's demand for naval bottoms. In February 1941, President Roosevelt signed an emergency naval appropriations bill authorizing an expenditure of nearly one billion dollars for new construction. While most of these funds were earmarked for large units to be built in coastal shipyards, Great Lakes builders were able to win contracts for the construction of many of the smaller, auxiliary vessels, the provisions of the Rush–Bagot Agreement prohibiting naval construction on the lakes having again been suspended by mutual agreement. The *Marine Engineering and Shipping Review* reported in February 1941 that Great Lakes yards would build "several cutters, thirty-six 165-foot submarine chasers, thirty 110-foot chasers, twenty-four motor torpedo boats and 190 mine sweepers of various sizes and types," with funding authorized by the naval appropriations bill. By 15 March, lake shipyards were holding government contracts totaling nearly ninety million dollars.[29] Among the larger orders, Defoe Boat and Motor Works of Bay City, Michigan was to build two subchasers, twelve escort vessels, four minesweepers and three tugs at a total value of sixteen million dollars, while smaller but significant contracts were awarded to Lake Superior Shipbuilding Company of Superior; Marine Iron and Shipbuilding Company of Duluth; and Sturgeon Bay Shipbuilding and Drydock Company, Peterson Boat Works, and Leatham Smith Ship Building Company, all of Sturgeon Bay, Wisconsin. In addition to these military orders, the Great Lakes yards also enjoyed a boom in repair work for the revitalized bulk fleet, while the American Shipbuilding Company of Lorain, Ohio, and the Great Lakes Engineering Works of River Rouge, Michigan, began work on twenty-one new ore carriers ordered by Pittsburgh Steamship Company and the U.S. Maritime Commission (see chapter 6).[30]

While the war had brought an abrupt end to the Depression in the Great Lakes bulk shipping industry, its effect on shipbuilding on the lakes was even more pronounced. By the end of 1941, shipyards around the lakes were working to apparent capacity, but the seemingly endless flow of military orders from Washington would soon bring expansion and innovation that would raise production beyond any previous levels.

3
1942-1945: Quotas and Controversy

Of course the great item . . . was the movement of iron ore on the Great Lakes. There is no transportation movement in the country which is more vital to the whole war effort, and the ore carriers have done an outstanding piece of work in bringing it to totals far beyond any previous records.
—Joseph B. Eastman, Director of Defense Transportation, 1943

In the wake of the attack on Pearl Harbor, President Roosevelt instituted a house cleaning in production management that many of his critics thought long overdue. On 16 January 1942, he finally named a production "czar," appointing Sears, Roebuck, and Company executive Donald Nelson as head of a new agency, the War Production Board (WPB), which replaced the OPM. Nelson was granted sweeping power to "exercise general direction over the nation's war procurement and production program and to determine the policies, plans, procedures, and methods of Government agencies in respect to war procurement and production." The Transportation Division of the NDAC had been abolished on 18 December 1941 and replaced with the Office of Defense Transportation (ODT), which was granted authority "over all railroads, motor vehicles, inland waterways, pipe lines, air transport, and coastwise and intercoastal shipping within the continental United States." This agency fell under the supervision of the WPB. Joseph B. Eastman was named director of ODT, and he recruited A. T. Wood into government service in the position of assistant director on Great Lakes carriers.[1]

In a most revealing letter to Wood dated 16 April 1942, Eastman addressed the goals for the coming season in a manner that would characterize the relationship between the federal government and the Great Lakes shipping industry throughout the war years. Following notice that the WPB had certified a goal of eighty-eight million gross tons of iron ore for 1942, he urged the vessel operators to take "voluntary action" to meet this target. After outlining several specific steps that should be taken, including the release of ships from less essential trades, Eastman closed the letter with a firm reminder of the power of his office: "I should greatly prefer, of course, that this ore movement be made and the goal of the certification attained without the necessity of any governmental intervention, but I think it must be said that legal means are at hand and if their use is necessary will be used."[2]

The threat implied by Eastman's letter was lost neither on Wood nor on the fleet owners, who wanted to retain operating control of their ships, and a meeting of representatives of all of the companies operating in the Great Lakes bulk shipping industry was immediately scheduled for Cleveland on 24 April. Here, the owners elected seven of their members to form the Lake Vessel Committee (LVC), "constituted for the purpose of providing maximum utilization of the Great Lakes fleet, in accordance with directive of Hon. Joseph B. Eastman, Director, Office of Defense Transportation." Karl H. Suder, chief traffic officer of the Akron, Canton, and Youngstown Railway, was given a leave of absence from that position to accept the office of director for the new committee, which would function as the principal agent of the LCA in dealing with the government for the balance of the war years.[3]

Now that the organizational framework was in place, the first goal of the new committee was to develop plans for meeting the eighty-eight-million-ton iron ore quota set by the WPB for the coming season. This quota would represent a 10 percent increase over the tonnage delivered in 1941, when the industry had been blessed by favorable weather and had operated at what appeared to be near capacity for the entire season. On 4 May 1942, D. C. Potts of the Pittsburgh Steamship Company, chairman of the LVC Ore and Vessel Subcommittee, prepared a memorandum that utilized the 1941 movement as a base amount and detailed seven measures proposed to increase the 1942 total—the two most important of which involved curtailment of grain and coal shipment in vessels capable of hauling iron ore. During the closing months of the 1941 season, some of the American iron ore fleet had abandoned the ore trade to move Canadian grain when the price for shipping a bushel of grain had skyrocketed from the normal two cents to eight cents. This practice was particularly obnoxious to Eastman, who had stated in his 16 April letter to Wood: "It is both improper and embarrassing for United States vessels to engage in the Canadian grain trade, which, I understand, is more profitable than the ore trade, while Canadian vessels are transporting our ore. This practice must be brought to an end." Potts estimated in his memorandum that a flat prohibition of grain movement in vessels capable of hauling ore would result in a two-million-gross-ton increase for the 1942 season. Office of Defense Transportation Order No. 8, effective 15 May 1942, effectuated this proposal by prohibiting all grain shipments in vessels of more than one thousand tons suited to the transportation of iron ore other than by special permit. The grain previously moved down the lakes by freighter was consigned to railroad transportation.[4]

Simultaneously, the ODT also took measures to restrict the lake movement of coal with the issuance of its Order No. 9, which prohibited Great Lakes bulk carriers from transporting coal "destined to points on the Detroit and St. Clair Rivers south of, and including Port Huron, Mich., or destined for transshipment through Lake Erie ports to other Lake Erie ports, or to points on Lake Ontario, or in the Chicago area." This order curtailed the time-consuming (but profit-enhancing) industry practice of dropping off a load of coal on an indirect route back up the lakes, but it did not completely prohibit the movement of coal by return trip. Again, the railroads were expected to pick up the slack in moving this commodity, a measure that Potts estimated would result in an annual increase of 2,175,000 gross tons of iron ore. Other measures relied upon to increase the season total included the early opening of navigation, deeper loading of ships, increased participation of Canadian boats, the utilization of five new freighters being built for the Pittsburgh Steamship Company (see chapter 6), and the reconstruction of automobile carriers to make them suitable for the ore trade. The War Shipping Administration (WSA) had purchased five vessels from the Nicholson Transit Company after conversion of the auto industry to wartime production had left these ships without a product to deliver; and these boats would add some 800,000 tons of carrying capacity to the fleet for the 1942 season.[5]

The initial 1942 season quota of 88,000,000 tons of ore was in place for less than a month when the shortage of ocean shipping forced the WPB to raise the amount needed to 89,500,000 tons. While the vast majority of all of the iron ore consumed in the United States was mined in the upper Midwest, a small portion had actually been imported from South America during the prewar era. Because of the location of its Sparrows Point production facility on the Maryland shore of the Chesapeake Bay, the Bethlehem Steel Corporation had imported 2,479,000 tons of ore—predominantly from Chile and to a lesser extent from Brazil and Cuba—during 1940. Given the availability of Lake Superior ore, the WPB decided that the scarce shipping tonnage used to supply the Sparrows Point plant could be better employed in the transportation of South American nitrate, copper, and bauxite, materials not as easily replaced from domestic sources. The Sparrows Point ore would arrive by rail from a southern lake port, while the foreign ore would be utilized by the British.[6]

Fortunately, the industry was again blessed with a mild spring that allowed the earliest season opening on record, the steamer *J. H. Sheadle* clearing Marquette on 23 March with a load of iron ore bound for Cleveland; by the end of March, tonnage figures were in excess of 700,000. However, the vagaries of early-season navigation on the lakes were apparent in April as falling temperatures created havoc on Lake Superior's Whitefish Bay and the St. Marys River. On 3 April, an ice blockade formed in the bay, prohibiting the movement of boats in either direction; and soon, as many as 120 ships were stuck, and 4 were reported aground. After this impediment was overcome, floating ice chunks jammed around the lock doors, disrupting their use for downbound traffic by delaying lockage to one ship per hour and causing some eighty ships to be delayed above the locks; normal operations were not resumed until 20 April.[7]

Despite the ice problems, the total iron ore shipped in April exceeded the record set in 1941, and the records continued to fall with each succeeding month. In October 1942, after the WPB again increased the iron-ore quota, this time to 91.5 million gross tons, the ODT issued General Order No. 25, which placed all Great Lakes ships under government control with all cargos authorized by general or special ODT permit. Under the authority of Order No. 25, the ODT could "direct the service of affected craft in any manner which the agency believed necessary for the preferential movement of war materials." This order was issued after the WPB set up a system of shipping priorities, with iron ore given the highest designation of A-1; but it had little effect on the Great Lakes, since virtually all craft capable of carrying the ore were already in service under the authority of the prior orders restricting the grain and coal movements.[8]

In order to meet the enormous iron ore quota, men and machinery had to operate at peak efficiency. As the ship pulled up to the dock, "those guys on the Huletts were all up there ready to go, all warmed up," the unloading commenced as soon as the boat was tied. Engines and boilers took a tremendous pounding, and maintenance procedures that would have laid up a ship for several days during quieter times were performed "on the run" whenever possible. Load-line limits were virtually ignored as long as a vessel was not overloaded for the river drafts, adding significantly to the tonnage a ship could deliver with each trip.[9]

As winter approached, the pace of the iron ore movement began to slow in the face of rapidly deteriorating weather conditions. Freezing temperatures were reported on the upper lakes as early as 2 September, and the time-consuming process of steaming the ore began at Duluth on 19 October. The LCA estimated that some fifty thousand railroad cars containing 4.5 million gross tons of ore were steamed and that the activity "was so constant that high-school boys voluntarily aided in the process." On 9 December, the

Edward Y. Townsend left Marquette with the season's final cargo, bringing the total iron ore movement for 1942 to a record-smashing 92,076,781 gross tons. Total shipments of all bulk commodities reached 178,587,397 net tons, a 6 percent increase over 1941; but as a result of the ODT restrictions, coal shipments were down slightly—grain shipments, significantly—from the prior year.[10]

As the highly successful 1942 shipping season was drawing to a close, the weather struck a tragic late-season blow, this time on Lake Erie, with the worst loss of life that lake had seen in more than a quarter of a century. The 130-ton tug *Admiral*, manned with a crew of fourteen, had left Toledo bound for Cleveland pulling the 250-foot barge *Cleveco* and her twenty four thousand barrels of oil. The tug and her tow were approaching Cleveland harbor early in the morning of 2 December in high seas and swirling snow when a watchman on the *Cleveco* realized that the *Admiral* had disappeared. The tug had simply gone down without warning, taking her entire crew to their deaths in the frigid water. Aboard the now helpless barge, the eighteen-man crew radioed for help but mistakenly gave their position as "off Avon Point." The Coast Guard concentrated rescue efforts in this area but were unable to locate the barge in the snowstorm. It was not until the following day that the crew of the cutter *Ossipee* spotted the *Cleveco* at a spot far distant from that originally reported; but the cutter could not maintain contact in the poor visibility, and the barge was not contacted again. It is believed that *Cleveco* sank late in the day on 3 December. All thirty-two sailors aboard the vessels were lost.[11]

During the 1942 season, requisitions by the War Shipping Administration had a significant impact on the package freight and passenger components of the lake fleet. As shipping losses mounted in the North Atlantic, WSA officials cast about desperately for replacement tonnage. The remaining Great Lakes package ships were still an obvious choice, because their 'tween-deck construction made them unsuitable for bulk cargos, while their small dimensions permitted transit through the Welland Canal and the St. Lawrence. All fourteen ships of the Great Lakes Transit Corporation were requisitioned in July of 1942, and their departure for ocean service effectively ended American-flag participation in the package freight business. While the ships were offered back to their prior owner after the war, rail and highway competition made their operation economically impractical, and they were sold to foreign operators. The WSA also drafted twenty small bulk freighters into ocean service, many of which served as colliers along the East Coast, freeing larger ships for trans-Atlantic runs. The Canadian government, too, was busy raiding the lakes for desperately needed bottoms, as that nation's Great Lakes fleet of canal-sized ships dropped from 136 to 73.[12]

In addition to the package fleet, the WSA also requisitioned two of the largest passenger ships on the lakes for a truly unique purpose. Following the attack on Pearl Harbor, the navy was faced with the problem of training thousands of new pilots in the perilous art of aircraft carrier landings. The Great Lakes Naval Air Station at Chicago provided an ideal location, since ships could operate on the waters of Lake Michigan without the danger of enemy submarine attacks. It was, however, physically impossible to bring an enormous carrier into the lakes even if one of these strategically irreplaceable vessels had been available for training purposes. On 14 March 1942, the navy announced the acquisition of the giant passenger liner *Seeandbee* from the Cleveland and Buffalo Steamship Company and detailed plans to convert the five-hundred-foot ship into a freshwater aircraft carrier. In the conversion process, all of the palatial upper superstructure was removed, the four stacks were shifted to the side, a flight deck was erected, and the ship was rechristened the USS *Wolverine*. A similar fate was met by the 535-foot *Greater Buffalo*, which joined the *Wolverine* as the USS *Sable*. Neither of the vessels was equipped to store or refuel aircraft, but they did provide adequate platforms for some fifteen thousand pilots who flew in from air bases around the lakes to practice landings and takeoffs on the pitching flight decks. Each trainee had to complete eight round trips in order to qualify as a carrier aviator and "A prime collection of naval aircraft from unsuccessful sorties still adorns the bottom of Lake Michigan."[13]

Despite the loss of the *Seeandbee* and the *Greater Detroit*, passenger ship operators did exceptionally well in 1942 and, indeed, throughout the war years, became several circumstances combined to make this era the final hurrah for Great Lakes excursion vessels. For the first time since the 1920s, large numbers of consumers had extra cash to spend on a vacation, while gas rationing and tire shortages all but eliminated competition from the automobile. As early as June 1941, the excursion companies were targeting war workers as the Detroit and Cleveland Navigation Company announced a "program of cruises and short week-end and holiday trips on the breeze-swept Great Lakes, designed to provide rest and relaxation to fit into the schedule of even the busiest of defense workers." In addition to regular, overnight runs across Lake Erie, the line offered weekend and holiday trips to Mackinac Island, as well as midweek trips to Georgian Bay and Harbor Springs. The Georgian Bay Line, operating the beautiful, white-hulled *North American* and *South American*, advertised one-week cruises from Detroit to Chicago or Duluth starting at $69.50 per person, while those on tighter budgets could cruise from Detroit to the Bob-Lo Island amusement park for a round-trip fare of sixty cents. There was no lack of takers as newspapers reported a "booming season," with accommodations at a premium.[14]

In 1943, the Georgian Bay Line invited travelers, "Conserve gas rubber and vital transportation facilities, this year take an approved 'V-cation' on the Great Lakes." The Detroit and Cleveland Line appealed to war workers with a takeoff on the military's famous "E" award for excellence in production, advertising "Ease, Entertainment, Eats, Excitement, Elation, Exhilaration, Enjoyment, Economy, Etc." on a boat trip to Buffalo. The pitch to production workers was highly successful: the company reported a 58 percent increase in passenger revenues over the preceding year and paid a dividend for the first time since 1931. On 15 June 1944, the *Cleveland Press*, in a sidebar to an article extolling the virtues of "patriotic vacations" on the Great Lakes, warned those intrepid souls considering an overland vacation to beware: "You may suddenly find trains and reservations cancelled to strand you in some far away spot. You will probably be forced to stand for long stretches in crowded railway cars. You will be caught in the rush of invasion traffic with the nation's trains and busses loaded to capacity." With the competition painted with such bleak strokes, it is easy to see why the Great Lakes passenger liners enjoyed a record season in 1942 and throughout the war years.[15]

As the 1942 shipping season came to an end on the Great Lakes, Americans were marking the close of their first full year of war. United States troops (and their equipment) were facing a baptism of fire against German forces in North Africa, while the bloody fighting on and around Guadalcanal was the focus of the war in the Pacific. On the home front, the "arsenal of democracy" was beginning to hit its stride, but the production effort was not without problems. By the end of June 1942, nearly half of the total American industrial output was war materiel; by July, plane production had hit one thousand per week, and merchant ships were being launched at the rate of three per week. As impressive as these accomplishments were, they still were short of goals and projections, and the overall production effort was plagued by problems of balance—oversupply in some areas and critical shortages in others. Much of the production output was "for the shelf," since the American military effort had still not placed large numbers of troops in the field against the Axis powers. Against this background, the demand for iron ore would continue into 1943; preliminary estimates put the goal at one hundred million gross tons. But while the 1942 season had been a story of accomplishment and success, the 1943 season would see frustration and failure.[16]

The first indication of the troubles that would plague the new season involved the difficulties presented by early-season ice conditions on the upper lakes. In an effort to duplicate the successful March and April shipments of the previous year, the ODT ordered an all-out ice-breaking effort in the spring of 1943; but adverse weather conditions stymied these ventures. The steamer *Philip D. Block* opened Escanaba on 4 April. But shortly thereafter, a cold wave and wind shift closed off the harbor, as well as the Straits of Mackinac; and a battle between man and ice that would last for forty days was under way. Windrowed ice in Whitefish Bay was reported to be thirty feet thick, forming a virtually impenetrable barrier that choked off shipments from Lake Superior ports for weeks; ore-loading docks in Duluth, Superior, and Marquette did not load their initial cargos until 24 April. By the end of that month, total iron-ore tonnage delivered stood at 1,954,817, compared to 8,649,708 for the previous season, a deficit that the industry would spend the entire year struggling to overcome.[17]

At a meeting of the LVC held in Cleveland on 19 April, the threat to season quotas posed by the ice conditions was recognized as the committee resisted pressure from the WPB to provide detailed projections of the amount of each bulk cargo that could be handled during the 1943 season. The committee recommended a reduction in the iron ore quota by one million gross tons due to an unexpected surplus in actual stocks on hand as of 1 April and further suggested that temporary blanket permits be issued to allow the transportation of all cargos in the same amounts as 1942, pending a complete review of the bulk cargo situation by the appropriate subcommittees. The only exception was a further restriction on coal shipments, under the previous year's Order No. 9, to 80 percent of that transported in 1942. Following the meeting, Wood told the press that the delay in opening navigation "may hamper realization of the [iron ore] goal this year." On 4 May, the LVC met again to consider the iron ore quota in light of the late opening of navigation; and the decision was made to lower the goal from ninety-five million to ninety-one million gross tons, reporting "This whole matter has been discussed with representatives of the Steel Division of the War Production Board with the view to determining the amount that the original directive . . . could be reduced without endangering steel production for the war effort."[18]

The discussions concerning goal reduction early in 1943 demonstrate the realities of the relationship between the government and the Great Lakes shipping industry during the war years. The existence of "quotas" set by the WPB gives the impression of a monolithic government agency directing compliance from a particular segment of the economy. In fact, the industry itself had much to do with generating these quotas when informing the WPB of the amount of iron ore that it was possible to deliver. The reduction suggested at the 4 May meeting took the form of a resolution that "recommends to Mr. A. T. Wood, Director, Great Lakes Carriers' Division, Office of Defense Transportation for submission to the War Production Board," that the quota be reduced. By the next meeting of the LVC, on 14 May, that "recommendation" had been adopted by the WPB and was now referred to as the "WPB directive that 91,000,000 gross tons of iron ore be transported via the Great Lakes during 1943." It is apparent that the WPB was, in fact, relying upon the LVC—and thus the industry itself—to determine the maximum goal that could realistically be met and then placing its weight and authority behind realization of that goal. A similar relationship existed with the ODT, whose Orders No. 8, 9, and 25 appeared to grant that agency complete control over the shipping industry. Resolutions were passed at the LVC meeting of 14 May, recommending that two steamers be allowed to carry grain until 15 June and that vessels delayed in Buffalo harbor by ice conditions be allowed to carry grain on their first trips up the lakes. These examples demonstrate that the LVC was in fact administering the ODT orders— that the industry was, for the most part, self-directed.[19]

Following receipt of the subcommittee reports, the LVC met again on 19 May to consider measures necessary to meet the new ninety-one-million-ton iron ore directive. One of the most significant problems posed to the shippers was a requirement of the Food Distribution Administration, subsequently approved by the WPB, that the American lake fleet transport some 135 million bushels of grain for 1943, 25 million more than the prior year, including 29 million bushels between 1 June and 15 September. The decision of the previous year to prohibit the involvement of certified ore vessels in the grain trade had resulted in an enormous backup of supply in grain elevators throughout the Great Lakes region, and the participation of the fleet was necessary to relieve the problem. While 10 million bushels of the midsummer total could be handled by smaller, noncertified craft, the remainder would have to be moved in the larger ships and would result in the loss of some six hundred thousand tons of ore capacity during the summer months. It was the recommendation of the LVC "that strong representations should be made to the effect that this grain cannot be moved in United States vessels without seriously affecting iron ore shipments." The same meeting also resulted in the submission of a dozen other proposals to the WPB, including a limitation on limestone shipments to provide for zero inventories in the hands of consumers by 1 May 1944. The minutes of the 2 June meeting of the LVC indicate that all of these recommendations were issued as directives by the WPB, with the exception of the elimination of the grain shipment requirement, which remained in effect. This latter decision of the WPB marked one of the few occasions during the war years when a recommendation of the LVC was not followed, and the resultant diversion of vessel capacity to the grain trade undoubtedly contributed to the failure of the industry to meet its iron ore quotas during the 1943 season.[20]

The months of June through September normally find the Great Lakes blessed with excellent sailing weather and the expectation of the industry was that some of the deficit caused by the late opening of navigation could be made up, particularly with the gradual addition to the fleet of the sixteen new freighters built by the U.S. Maritime Commission (see chapter 6). However, these hopes were dashed by an almost unbelievable string of foggy days, accidents, and bad luck. Great Lakes freighters were not equipped with radar until the closing days of World War II, so fog was, and always had been, a deadly peril, particularly in the narrow channels of the St. Marys, St. Clair and Detroit Rivers and the Straits of Mackinac. While the crews could navigate by dead reckoning on the waters of the open lake, this process would not work in the channels, where precision was required. The unusually cold water temperatures, resulting from the late spring, combined with the warm June air to produce a series of dense fogs that hung over the lakes for days. With the constant pressure to deliver the iron ore, the ships kept moving whenever possible, with predictable results.

During the first three days of June, a strange series of collisions and groundings involved ten separate vessels and sent a half-dozen to the shipyards for repairs. On 1 June, the 640-foot Pittsburgh Steamship Company freighter *Irving S. Olds* and the 530-foot *C. O. Jenkins* of the Midland Steamship Company were damaged in a collision attributed to dense fog on Lake Erie, while another collision on Lake Ontario sent the Canadian steamer *Prindoc* to the bottom. On the following day, the *W. W. Holloway* rammed the *Harry W. Hosford* in dense fog near Whitefish Point; the captain of the *Hosford* was able to save his ship by driving her on the beach with her deck just barely out of the water. After a brief respite, the fog returned again at midmonth, and more misfortune followed. On 15 June, the steamer *George M. Humphrey* sank in the Straits of Mackinac after a collision with the *Clemson*, taking twelve thousand tons of ore to the bottom with her, while another collision later that same day sank the British grain vessel *Brewster* in the St. Clair River off Algonac and disabled the ore freighter *W. D. Caverly, Jr.** A third collision later that week on the St. Marys River involving the 621-foot ore carrier *Frank Armstrong* and the Canadian ship *Goderich* was also attributed to the fog.[21]

The operating delays caused by the fog and the loss of capacity due to the rash of accidents crippled the efforts of the fleet to overcome the iron ore

---

*The loss of the *Humphrey* set the stage for one of the great salvage stories in Great Lakes history. Captain John Roen of Sturgeon Bay headed a crew that first brought up the twelve thousand tons of ore from a depth of seventy feet, then the ship itself, despite the swift currents of the strait. The salvaged vessel returned to service during the 1945 season as the *Captain John Roen*.

deficit occasioned by the late opening of navigation, and it was soon apparent to the LVC and the WPB that the quotas set were not attainable. As early as 2 June, the LVC minutes reveal a concern to assure that all iron ore customers would be treated equally in sharing any deficit; and a detailed survey of consumers was initiated to determine the amount of ore already delivered to each, so that shortages could be apportioned. At an LVC meeting in early July, committee member Elton Hoyt II reported that the deficit had dominated his recent discussions with production officials in Washington and that the WPB had been preparing a consumer survey similar to that already undertaken by the LVC. A letter from H. Van B. Cleveland, deputy chief of the Transportation Branch of the WPB, dated 3 July, pessimistically reported that "it was the opinion of the (Lake Vessel) Committee that . . . a movement of 87,000,000 gross tons of ore . . . seemed all that was probable."[22]

While the bulk shippers were struggling to meet quotas on the lakes, the shooting war in the Atlantic was continuing to claim veterans of past lake service. On 27 May, the *Jack* was torpedoed while carrying sugar from Puerto Rico to New Orleans—the little vessel went to the bottom in less than five minutes. Several members of her crew were rescued after spending thirty-two days adrift on a life raft. On 18 June, boat watchers around the lakes were stunned to learn of the loss of the U.S. Coast Guard cutter *Escanaba* to an enemy torpedo attack. The 165-foot ship had been built for Great Lakes service at the Defoe yard in Bay City and had spent its first ten years stationed at Grand Haven, Michigan. In late 1941, the vessel had sailed to Manitowoc for extensive alterations, and she departed the lakes in May 1942 for a new career escorting convoys on the North Atlantic. Only two sailors from the ship's complement of 103 men survived the sinking.[23]

As the difficult summer dragged on, the accidents that had frustrated the bulk shipping industry continued. On 15 July, the *Irving S. Olds,* one of the five giant new Pittsburgh Steamship freighters, was damaged for the second time in just six weeks in a collision with the sandsucker *John M. McKerchey* in the Detroit River. The last week of July saw fog cause three ships to run aground in the St. Marys River, disrupting downbound traffic. On 30 September, fog caused the grounding of the *Henry Ford II* and the *Frank Purnell* in the St. Clair River off Marine City; and a collision in Sandusky Harbor on 13 October caused the death of a crewman aboard the *A. M. Byers.* While summarizing the problems encountered by the industry, the *Wall Street Journal* reported that fog had slowed shipping on 51 of 122 days from May to October and that deliveries of 1.7 to 2 million tons of ore had been lost to holdups at the Soo Locks alone. In addition to weather-related problems, the cooperation of the Canadian fleet in the iron ore movement was less than expected, because the demand for coal and grain delayed the participation of these vessels. During the closing months of the season, some of the ships certified to carry iron ore were diverted to the grain movement in order to meet the quotas established for that commodity, and it became apparent that even the reduced quota of 86.5 million tons set on 3 August would not be met.[24]

One lake veteran with particularly vivid memories of the 1943 season is John LeCorn who, at the tender age of twenty-six, put in his first year as a Great Lakes captain aboard the *Tampico* of the Nicholson Transit Company.* The 247-foot *Tampico* had been requisitioned by the War Shipping Administration at the beginning of the 1942 season but was returned for lake service, along with thirteen other steamers, in the spring of 1943. Unfortunately for LeCorn, the *Tampico* that was returned was hardly the same stout little ship he had served on as a wheelsman and mate before the war. In order to adapt the vessel for runs along the Atlantic coast, the WSA had converted one of her four ballast tanks to hold fresh water and another for additional fuel storage. As a result the boat would bob like a cork atop the water when it was without a cargo, catching the wind like a sail. In addition to the ballast problem, the ship had been stripped of much of her equipment, including her gyrocompass and even her radio telephone. Arriving in Fort William, Ontario to pick up a load of grain, LeCorn would battle the wind coming off the lake to make a soft landing, then, because he still lacked a phone, he would have to send someone ashore to find out which elevator he was to load at, then cast off and make another adventurous landing elsewhere in the harbor.

While the physical condition of the *Tampico* presented problems for her new skipper, they paled in comparison to those occasioned by her "1943 crew." Manpower shortages plagued the industry throughout the war years (see chapter 5), but they were particularly acute on vessels like the *Tampico*. Larger vessels that had operated in previous seasons had at least a cadre of trained officers and men who could teach and cover for new recruits. This was not the case for many of the smaller boats pressed into service by the war, especially the group of ships returned to the lakes by the WSA, where entire crews had to be assembled from scratch.

LeCorn was given a competent chief engineer; but after that, the pickings were slim. His second mate held only a Mississippi River license, while a third mate got drunk and refused to leave his room. Several of the wheels-

---

*When the youthful LeCorn was fitting out his new command in Buffalo harbor that spring, a gray-haired fellow approached him on the deck and asked, "Hey kid, can you tell me where the captain is?"

men simply did not know how to make a turn; and on many occasions, Le-Corn had to grab the wheel on the St. Marys River to avoid disaster. Similar problems existed on the after end. After backing out of the Nicholson slip in Detroit one day, LeCorn signaled the engine room to proceed forward, but the ship just kept backing straight for the steel mill. LeCorn sounded the ships whistle to alert the chief and quickly dropped the anchor. The chief raced to the engine room to find the intoxicated assistant oblivious to his surroundings. Not even the galley was exempt from the problems. When the fire in the stove went out, the cook called the captain, the only one aboard who knew how to light it!

Fortunately, LeCorn and his ship survived the 1943 season without a major incident: "It was a madhouse. All we did was survive. It was a good thing I was twenty-six, there's no getting around that, I'd have likely died!"[25]

As the end of the season approached, one further innovation was utilized in the effort to maximize iron ore shipments: the federal government participated in providing insurance for vessels operating into December. Commercial underwriters increased their premiums every three days after the last day of November, so that a ship operating into the third week of December would pay as much for the December coverage as for the entire regular season. To solve this problem, the ODT requested that the War Shipping Administration (WSA) underwrite normal commercial insurance through its Division of Wartime Insurance, allowing the shippers to pay normal rates during December, with the government functioning as a guarantor for the insurance companies. While this innovation did allow the movement of some iron ore during December, it had a very limited effect as extremely cold weather quickly closed down activity on the upper lakes, with the last cargo of iron ore departing Duluth on 7 December.[26]

During the 1943 season, the Great Lakes shipping industry delivered 84,404,852 gross tons of iron ore and 175,652,684 net tons of all bulk cargos —amounts significantly less than those carried during 1942 and far below season-opening quotas. The failure of the industry to reach its goals was due almost entirely to the problems of ice and fog, since all nine iron ore loading facilities functioned on only 224 days, as compared with 251 days during the 1942 season. Fortunately, the shortfall in iron ore deliveries had no effect on steel production, since the LVC program of apportioning the deficit among the various consumers was successful and the producers were able to draw upon their stockpiles to meet demand. In early February 1944, 36,000,000 tons of ore were still available; and with monthly consumption averaging 7,500,000 tons, this constituted a sufficient reserve until the opening of the new navigation season.[27]

American war production peaked in November of 1943, when some six billion dollars' worth of guns, tanks, ships, and munitions flowed from the nation's factories and shipyards; two-thirds of the nation's industrial output was generated for the war effort. By the summer of 1944, millions of superbly equipped American troops were fighting in France; and sufficient quantities of munitions were in reserve to allow the beginnings of a reconversion movement. Yet reconversion to a peacetime economy would prove difficult. Big business was opposed to a gradual reconversion because of a fear that small enterprises would have an advantage in meeting pent up consumer demand, while the military would not tolerate a slackening of homefront restrictions at a time when casualty figures were rising every week. The dispute centered in the WPB, where Donald Nelson's efforts to begin a gradual reconversion program eventually led to his resignation; and the production effort continued unabated. In 1944, "the country was working overtime to produce surplus and scrap for the postwar era."[28]

The minutes of the early meetings of the LVC during the 1944 season demonstrate that the crisis atmosphere of the prior year was not to be repeated. The iron ore quota was set at eighty-four million tons, an amount sufficient to replace consumption for the twelve-month period ending 1 April 1944. While ice conditions were difficult, the problems of 1943 were not repeated, and the first cargo was loaded at Escanaba on 4 April. By the end of the month, more than five million tons had been shipped, a comfortable margin upon which to build. With a full season expected from the sixteen new Maritime Class freighters, over four million tons additional capacity was also available (see chapter 6). Even after allowances were made for significantly increased grain and coal movement, the LVC still projected a two-million-ton surplus over the eighty-four-million-ton iron ore quota.[29]

On 27 April, fog caused two collisions in Lake Erie: one sent the ore carrier *James H. Reed* to the bottom with the loss of ten of her crew, while the other saw the foundering of the *Frank E. Vigor*. The sinking of these two ships meant a loss of 405,000 tons of annual carrying capacity for the iron ore fleet. Fortunately, these accidents did not mark a trend like that seen in 1943: the balance of the sailing season featured remarkably pleasant weather, with the industry functioning smoothly in pursuit of its shipping goals. Given the ample iron ore capacity, the previous restrictions on coal shipments were delayed until 15 July; and American ships moved nearly 50 percent of the lake grain cargos, a level of participation in that commodity never before seen. Mild temperatures in the fall allowed the vessels to operate well into December; but for the first time since 1938, no iron ore was shipped in that month, sufficient quantities having already been delivered to allow a concentration of vessel capacity in the grain trade. The total iron ore shipments for the 1944 season amounted to 81,170,538 gross tons, while total net tonnage for all bulk commodities reached an all-time high of 184,159,492. This figure included 16,228,880 net tons of grain, the largest total transported on the lakes since 1928.[30]

As the beginning of the 1945 season approached, the LVC was informed "[that the] Armed Services were making increased demands for steel from the Industry and that for the second quarter of this calendar year a definite shortage in steel was apparent, which indicated a continued necessity for maximum shipment of iron ore." Ground storage of ore as of 1 April was predicted at sixteen million tons, and a quota of eighty-three million tons for the season was thought to be sufficient to replace actual consumption. In addition to the demands for iron ore, shippers were also informed that the American fleet would be expected to move some 340 million bushels of grain, a 15 percent increase over the amount shipped during the 1944 season. When the LVC met again on 9 May, they heard the first indication that demand for iron ore might soon slacken, when it was reported that a survey of consumers indicated actual needs at eighty-one million tons and that "this was a maximum tonnage and might be subject to further decrease in the event that production of steel should be less than capacity during the present shipment year."[31]

Record-breaking warm temperatures during the month of March dissolved the ice on the upper lakes, allowing an easy and early opening of navigation, with the *Peter Reiss* carrying the season's first load of ore out of Escanaba on 2 April. As of 15 May, 270 of 287 vessels certified as ore carriers were actually operating in the ore trade, with the balance moving grain. The fleet continued to move ore at a rate sufficient to meet its quota through the summer months, until the cessation of hostilities brought a cancellation of orders in the late summer and early fall. Despite the softening of demand for ore, bulk shippers were still operating at capacity to meet the unprecedented demand for grain movement in the fall of the year. United States and Canadian farmers were completing the second consecutive year of record wheat harvests, while demand for export wheat to feed the prostrate nations of Europe was at an all-time high. Relatively mild weather on the upper lakes allowed the continuous operation of the fleet well into December, with the last ore cargo departing from Escanaba on 5 December and the last grain cargo from Duluth on 9 December. The season total for iron ore shipments was 75,714,750 gross tons, while the total of all bulk cargos was 175,083,683 net tons, the outstanding feature of this total being the movement of a season record total of 18,717,773 net tons of grain.[32]

After the surrender of the Japanese, the LVC was informed that the ODT Office of the Great Lakes Carriers Division was to close as of 22 September 1945 and that all controls over the industry would cease as of that date. In

51

response, the LVC pointed out that much confusion would exist in the closing months of the season unless some form of control continued, particularly in light of the heavy grain demand; and the committee recommended
that Wood continue as consultant, Great Lakes Carriers Division until the
end of the navigation season. On 14 December 1945, Wood and all the
members of the LVC submitted their resignations to Colonel J. M. Johnson,
the new director of the ODT, thus formally bringing to an end government
authority over the industry.[33]

The overall performance of the Great Lakes bulk shipping industry during World War II was one of significant accomplishments in the face of
daunting adversity. These accomplishments were due, in no small measure,
to the efforts of the LCA, whose officers provided the leadership and expertise necessary to meet the extraordinary demand. During the seven shipping
seasons covered by this work, the industry delivered some 522,268,987 gross
tons of iron ore, a season average of 74,609,855 gross tons, or 9,400,000 tons
above the previous single-season record set in 1929. Simultaneously, the
fleet was delivering a season average of 164,194,166 net tons of all bulk cargos, as compared to the 1929 single-season record of 138,574,441 net tons.
More important than the statistics, however, was the fact that the United
States steel industry was able to produce the weapons of war without a single
interruption attributable to a lack of the raw materials supplied by the Great
Lakes fleet.

While the bulk carriers were amassing unprecedented totals, the Great
Lakes shipbuilders were making their own unique contributions to the nation's war effort. On 30 April 1942, the USS *Peto* slid sideways into the Manitowoc River, the first of the submarines to be launched under the government contract with the Manitowoc Shipbuilding Company. After fitting out
and test diving were completed on Lake Michigan the ship was delivered to
the navy by means of the Illinois Waterway–Mississippi River route.* Construction of a submarine posed some difficult problems for the inland shipyard, but innovative solutions were developed to meet them. The hull of the
Peto consisted of fifteen separate pieces that were built upside down, allowing the workers to utilize the far more consistent downward weld. When all
the pieces were ready they were rolled over by means of specially developed
cranes and welded together into a single hull. With the coming of hostilities,
the original contract for ten boats was soon expanded; and by war's end, the
company had produced a total of twenty-eight submarines along with thirty-
seven landing craft, fourteen minesweepers, and many smaller craft. The

*Between the submarine testing and the aircraft carrier landing operations, large
portions of Lake Michigan were off-limits to civilian traffic during the war years.

company also produced numerous shipyard cranes during the war years, including six that were completed in early 1942 under "mandatory priority" for use at Pearl Harbor.[34]

While the Manitowoc submarine contract was the most glamorous of the construction contributions, other yards around the Great Lakes were producing equally impressive numbers of military bottoms. At his Defoe Shipbuilding Company in Bay City, Michigan, Harry J. Defoe utilized a roll-over hull construction technique similar to that used at Manitowoc to produce fifty-eight 173-foot subchasers for the navy under a contract originally let in 1941. Defoe's method featured a single locomotive crane that could roll the completed hull over in five minutes' time with a crew of only a dozen men, and this successful innovation led to an October 1942 contract for the construction of the first saltwater surface combat ships to be built on the lakes. The first of these 307-foot destroyer escorts, the USS *Bull*, was begun in December 1942 and delivered down the Mississippi in August 1943; the company originally contracted to build twenty-eight of these ships, but the final eleven were delivered as fast transports. By early 1944, the yard was concentrating on production of the large landing craft so desperately needed for the coming European invasion; fifty-eight of these, including forty-two Landing Craft, Infantry (LCI), were eventually launched. At the height of wartime production, Defoe was employing some four thousand workers and meeting a monthly payroll in excess of one million dollars.[35]

A similar production miracle transformed the tiny Wisconsin city of Sturgeon Bay. Located halfway up the Door Peninsula on the eastern shore of Green Bay, the town of less than five thousand souls was home to the Leathem D. Smith Shipbuilding Company, a tiny enterprise with fifty employees and a monthly payroll of eight thousand dollars, when it was awarded its first government contract for the construction of four army tugs in December 1940. During the next five years, the company delivered ninety-seven ships to the armed services and the Maritime Commission with a total value in excess of $140,000,000, while employing 5,600 workers at a monthly payroll of $1,250,000. As with the Defoe yard, Smith sought to overcome a critical shortage of experienced shipbuilders by resorting to novel construction methods. Virtually all of the hulls were of welded, rather than riveted, construction, which allowed for the use of unskilled production-line workers assembling large, prefabricated sections in shops away from the actual launching berths. The sections were then delivered to the construction site, where they could be quickly welded together, thus greatly reducing the time between keel laying and launching. The Smith yard was also a leader in the employment of women in ship construction, utilizing over six hundred in welding, painting, and (particularly) the skilled trade of electrical wiring.[36]

By 1944, expansion at the yard had reached the point where the company was building as many as five different types of vessels simultaneously, including 173-foot subchasers and gunboats for the navy and 258-foot coasters, 305-foot frigates, and 340-foot cargo carriers for the Maritime Commission. The company was one of the few in the nation to receive both the army–navy "E" and the Maritime Commission "M" production awards. In addition to the Smith Company, Sturgeon Bay was also home to the Sturgeon Bay Shipbuilding and Drydock Company, Sturgeon Bay Boat Works, and Peterson Boat Works, companies that together produced another 130 smaller craft for the armed services.[37]

A similar concentration of shipbuilding facilities sprang up in the Duluth–Superior region surrounding the waters of St. Louis Bay. The Zenith Dredge and Marine Iron Works of Duluth constructed thirty-eight vessels for the U.S. Coast Guard including the 180-foot seagoing tenders *Acacia*, *Bramble*, *Mariposa*, *Mesquite*, *Sundew*, and *Woodrush*, all of which continued to serve on the Great Lakes for many years, while the Globe Shipbuilding Company of Superior built oceangoing tugs and 305-foot frigates for the navy. The Walter Butler Shipbuilding Company was the area's largest contributor, delivering some eighty-one vessels during the war years from its two yards on opposite sides of the bay. The company employed 4,250 people in the construction of twelve 305-foot frigates, twenty-seven three-thousand-ton coasters, and forty-two C1-M-AV1 cargo vessels. These last ships, at 340-feet, were the largest oceangoing craft built by Great Lakes contractors during the war years; and they were delivered down the Illinois Waterway–Mississippi River route with their deckhouses and masts disassembled and stowed on deck to allow clearance under fixed bridges.[38]

Robert Butler, owner of the Butler Shipbuilding Company, was the originator of one of the more interesting publicity stunts of the war years—a simultaneous launching of five new cargo vessels christened by the eight-year-old Dionne quintuplets. The decision to "drop five of 'em in on one day" was meant to dramatize the construction prowess of the Duluth–Superior region and the participation of the world-famous quintuplets, on their first tour of the United States, guaranteed a media circus. Admission to the ten-thousand bleacher seats constructed on the Butler yard was set at $3.30, and fifty thousand souvenir programs were printed for sale at $1 each. On Sunday, 9 May, the Dionne family arrived in Superior by train for the big event and were greeted by a crowd estimated at one hundred thousand people, including Emory S. Land, chairman of the Maritime Commission and Vice-Chairman H. L. Vickery, plus a national radio audience. Following some nineteen speeches (which the French–Canadian girls could not understand), the quints, dressed in matching gray suits and white blouses, broke bottles of Niagara Falls water over the bows of the ships and sent them sideways down the ramps. The only disappointment of the whole affair was the decision of the Maritime Commission to not allow the five ships to be named after Annette, Emilie, Yvonne, Cecile, and Marie. Pursuant to commission Order N-3, all of the vessels in this class had to be named for early American frigate captains, so the ships went to sea with the much more prosaic "monikers" of *Moses Gay, Guerdon Gates, Bailey Foster, Watson Ferris,* and *Asa Aldridge.*[39]

Other major contractors around the lakes included the American Shipbuilding Company of Cleveland, which, in addition to the Maritime Class bulk carriers (see chapter 6), built minesweepers and frigates; Froemming Brothers of Milwaukee, which built frigates and C1-M-AV1s; and Henry Grebe of Chicago, which built minesweepers and tankers.[40]

In addition to the construction of submarines and large surface craft, other Great Lakes companies turned out thousands of motor boats, utility vessels, and landing craft for the armed forces. Notable in this group was the contribution of the Chris-Craft Corporation of Algonac, Michigan, which, by 1940, was the world's largest producer of pleasure boats. Conversion to wartime production was not nearly as difficult for Chris-Craft as it was for some of the companies building larger vessels, since small-boat engineering and mass production techniques were already in existence at the company's three factories in Algonac, Cadillac, and Holland, Michigan. So rapid and successful was the changeover that the company was awarded the navy "E" on 18 June 1942. From 1942 to 1945, Chris-Craft produced over twelve thousand landing craft, most of which were thirty-six-foot-long Landing Craft Vehicle and Personnel (LCVP), Landing Craft Personnel, Large (LCP[L]), and Landing Craft Personnel, Ramped (LCP[R]). The company also produced harbor patrol picket boats and speedboats.[41]

It has been estimated that wartime shipbuilding contracts awarded to Great Lakes concerns totaled well in excess of one billion dollars and that some eight thousand prime contractors and subcontractors were utilized. While it is apparent that the size restrictions imposed on Great Lakes construction by the St. Lawrence Canals limited these contracts to the smaller, less glamorous ships of war, the successful fulfillment of these contracts by Great Lakes shipbuilders freed the coastal yards for larger construction and contributed greatly to the defeat of the Axis powers.[42]

4
Protecting the Lakes

The extreme importance of maintaining an uninterrupted flow of iron
ore from the mines in the Lake Superior Region to blast furnaces in
various industrial centers during the present national emergency is
readily apparent. . . . Although the primary responsibility for the safeguarding of the facilities of the various transportation concerns rests
with the individual ship operators, they may be assured of this Bureau's cooperation in assisting them to minimize the possibility of
sabotage or espionage affecting their facilities.
                                                —J. Edgar Hoover, 1941

J Edgar Hoover was just one of many Americans who recognized that the
long and tortuous shipping route from the northern ore ranges to the
midwestern steel plants was the jugular vein of the nation's war production effort. Given the relatively small amount of ground storage available,
any prolonged disruption of Great Lakes traffic would bring an eventual halt
to steel production, so measures had to be taken to protect the shipment of
bulk cargos from either direct attack or sabotage.

In the months following the outbreak of war in Europe, it was sabotage
that loomed as the larger threat. As we have seen, there were approximately
three hundred freighters operating in the iron ore trade at any time during
the war years. While the loss of individual vessels would not have had a crippling effect on the industry, the sinking of one or more ships in any one of
the several narrow channels of the system could have had disastrous consequences. This was particularly true of the Soo Locks, through which passed
over 90 percent of the iron ore shipments.

The initial impetus for the adoption of security measures to protect the
Great Lakes shipping industry came from representatives of the Canadian
government in the summer of 1940, that nation being actively involved as a
belligerent in the European conflict. On 17 June 1940, Canadian vessel owners promulgated a series of security rules governing loading procedures and
passages through canals controlled by the Canadian government. A copy of

57

these rules was forwarded to the Lake Carriers Association by the Royal Canadian Mounted Police, who requested that the LCA adopt similar measures to coordinate the security efforts on both sides of the border. In response, the LCA convened a meeting of its membership and representatives of the U.S. Army Corps of Engineers and the U.S. Coast Guard in Cleveland on 1 August.[1]

The resolution adopted by the LCA at that meeting set forth a set of rules to be followed by members of the association, as well as all other lake vessel operators who agreed to comply with its terms. Given that no governmental agency was, as of yet, exercising any direct control over the American fleet, the resolution was described as "voluntary and cooperative in an effort to avoid establishment of government regulations which might be more strict." The industry was successful in avoiding more stringent government control: the regulations promulgated in August 1940 remained in effect, with only minor alterations, throughout the war years. Pursuant to the new measures, the LCA instituted a shore-leave pass system that required all sailors to have in their possession a pass signed by an officer of the ship before leaving the vessel in port. Upon his return, the individual had to display the pass to the deck watch, as well as submit to a search of all parcels, including private luggage. Officers of the ship were also required to search the hold before cargo was taken on board and actually to observe and supervise the loading process so as to exclude the introduction of any explosive materials aboard the ship.[2]

Immediately after the freighter had left port, an officer was to conduct an extensive search of "all closed compartments, the fore peak and after peak, blind hold, dunnage room, windlass room, and chain locker" and was to enter such in the ship's log. A similar inspection was to be made before entering the Sault or Welland Canals; and the ship was to hoist a large, yellow flag with a black ball in the center, indicating the letter "I" in the International Signal Code, to notify officials at the locks that the inspection had been completed. No ship was to be granted passage without displaying the yellow flag.[3]

These inspection requirements would prove somewhat onerous to officers required to search every nook and cranny of their ships at frequent intervals; a review of available logbooks indicates that compliance throughout the war years was, at best, sporadic. The logbook of the steamer *Carmi A. Thompson* of the Midland Steamship Line, covering the years 1942–45, is instructive. During the 1942 season, handwritten entries such as "Inspected ship" or "Vessel inspected" appear in the log before each entry into the Soo Locks; but the book is without any such references for 1943 or 1944. In 1945, the crew began the regular use of the somewhat overblown phrase, "Entire ship inspected as per War Department Regulations for passage thru Soo

Locks," which would seem to indicate a shift in company policy toward compliance. The log of the Cleveland–Cliffs steamer *Champlain* shows the use of a rubber stamp with a listing of all of the areas to be searched as set forth in the regulations. The officer would simply stamp the log page, check off each compartment and enter the starting and ending times for the search. It is interesting to note that the total elapsed time for each search is ten to fifteen minutes, certainly not a great deal of time in which to make a thorough inspection of each compartment of a six-hundred-foot ore carrier; and it appears that as the war years dragged on, compliance was increasingly pro forma.[4]

Aboard ships of the Pittsburgh fleet, a company policy in effect long before the wartime regulations required the mate on duty to walk to the stern of the ship and inspect the steering gear on the fantail before the boat entered the locks. This practice was continued during the war years, but officers who sailed during those days readily admit that no effort was made to complete the type of search envisioned by the LCA regulations. Even hoisting the requisite inspection flag became a nuisance after many trips, and the sailors developed several ingenious methods to avoid this chore. Some simply left the flag up full-time; but the elements would soon wear out the pennant, so a more durable replacement was needed. Aboard one Pittsburgh ship, the crew painted a piece of scrap metal with the colors of the inspection flag and placed it above the pilot house when approaching the locks, while the mates aboard the *James J. Hill* went them one better by permanently fastening their painted piece of tin to the roof of the bridge.[5]

While it is apparent that a rather cavalier attitude existed toward the search requirements imposed by the LCA, in defense of the officers, real vessel security came from the tight and familiar relationships that existed on the lake freighters, where many of the crew members sailed together for years and where any suspicious behavior by an outsider would have quickly attracted attention.

In addition to preparing rules governing the protection of lake freighters, the LCA was also involved in efforts to safeguard the dock facilities of the industry. At a meeting convened in Cleveland on 12 July 1940, the LCA met with representatives of many of the dock operators of the Great Lakes region to discuss a proposal for the protection of shoreline installations. Lake Carriers Association president A. T. Wood chaired the meeting and explained to the group that a recent survey had found that the cost of fencing all of the shoreline facilities would be "prohibitive"; and the decision of the group was to institute a pass system similar to that to be utilized aboard ship. The point was emphasized that each dockowner bore the ultimate responsibility for safeguarding that particular installation and, with the exception of the pass system, no uniform regulations were adopted.[6]

The 1940 regulations paid particular attention to the highly vulnerable Soo Locks, which would become one of the most heavily guarded civilian installations in the United States. The first step in providing protection for the locks came as early as 26 August 1939, when British troops were posted at the locks and their approaches on the Canadian side. One week later, after Hitler's attack on Poland, the United States government announced that visitors would no longer be allowed at the locks on the American side. This decision would have significant consequences for the economy of the Sault Ste. Marie area, where thousands of tourists flocked during the summer months to watch the raising and lowering of the big freighters from a park immediately adjacent to the American locks. Also, on 3 September, a detachment of twenty soldiers from nearby Fort Brady was detailed to the locks, machine guns were set up on piers at both approaches, and snow fence barricades topped with barbed wire were installed to limit access. By 12 October, "anti-aircraft guns, machine guns, a battery of sky-piercing searchlights, squads of infantrymen, a small fleet of coast guard craft and miles and miles of new fence topped by barbed wire" were in place around the locks.[7]

During the spring of 1940, political pressure was being exerted in Washington by Senator Prentiss M. Brown and Representative Fred Bradley to lift the ban on visitors and thus preserve a good portion of the tourist trade of Michigan's Upper Peninsula. On 15 June, the military relented and the order barring visitors was lifted with the provision that all cameras, packages, and firearms had to be checked with guards before visitors were allowed to enter the lock area. Later that summer, the military reconsidered and again ordered the locks closed to visitors effective 12 August; but Brown and Bradley were able to have the order rescinded until 2 September, thus preserving the tourist traffic through the balance of the summer. In addition to banning visitors from the locks, the government also sought to eliminate the operation of concession, or "bum," boats, which traditionally met the freighters at the locks and supplied newspapers, laundry, and miscellaneous services to the ships. This order was also modified, primarily through the efforts of the LCA, with the government continuing to allow the operation of concession boats "under strict military supervision and control."[8]

During the months preceding the attack on Pearl Harbor, the issue of the safety and protection of the locks occasionally found its way into print. On 4 August 1940, the *Detroit Free Press* reported that Sault Ste. Marie civic leaders "pointed out . . . that it would be possible for enemy bombers to strike here from a base in Hudson Bay 600 miles to the north—only two hours by air"—a statement apparently made in an effort to obtain federal funding for the expansion of the local airport. On 10 February 1941, Coast Guard commandant R. R. Waesche testified before a House appropriations subcommittee in Washington that the locks were "a very vulnerable spot" and that the military was "considerably worried" about sabotage to the installation. While sabotage concerned Admiral Waesche, it was a direct attack that troubled Lieutenant Colonel Harold A. Furlong, who told a convention of the Michigan Bankers' Association that, "It is not beyond the ingenuity of Hitler's military schemers to carry bombing planes in sections across the Atlantic by submarine and slip them through the slim cordons of the naval patrols into the Hudson Bay area. There, on some lonely island, safe from the eyes of all except an occasional Indian, those planes could be reassembled and made ready for an attack on the Soo ship canal." On 15 February 1941, the task of guarding the locks was assigned to the 702d Military Police Battalion, a specially trained force of 546 officers and men under the authority of the U.S. Department of the Interior. Additional concerns for the safety of the St. Marys Falls Canal followed the railroad accident of October 1941, which vividly brought home the vulnerability of the entire shipping industry to any disruption occasioned by damage to the locks.[9]

In the weeks following the stunning air attack at Pearl Harbor, industry concern for the protection of the Soo Locks grew to near hysterical proportions; but it seemed that no one was listening. On 16 December, Wood wrote to Colonel August M. Krech of the U.S. Army, pointing out the need for additional antiaircraft defenses at the Soo and stating, "One point that cannot be too emphatically stressed is the absolute necessity of making certain beyond reasonable doubt that no acts of sabotage will be perpetrated at the St. Marys Falls Canal, Sault Ste. Marie, Michigan." In his response of 23 December, Krech outlined the defensive measures already undertaken at the Soo and assured Wood that "this possible contingency [air attack] has been given much consideration and such a possibility has been considered in our plans." Under different circumstances, such a vague assurance might well have sufficed; but in the charged atmosphere that followed the debacle of 7 December, a military assurance that all was well was not nearly enough to satisfy those concerned with the safety of the locks. On 29 December, Wood again wrote to the army, attempting to reemphasize the strategic importance of the locks and asking that "action looking toward the provision of anti-aircraft protection . . . be expedited.[10]

As the days passed without any apparent military efforts to increase defenses in the Sault Ste. Marie area, pressure from within the industry centered on Wood, as spokesman for the LCA, to "wake up" authorities in Washington. Wood was reminded that there was "a feeling of insecurity about the protection of the Soo Locks" and a necessity to "hammer away at this question until Washington knowingly assumes the full responsibility for whatever protection is given." On 8 January 1942, the president of the Gartland Steamship Company requested that Wood form a committee to address the issue and urged, "I cannot help but believe that Germany has an eye on this Soo situation and that either German saboteurs or perhaps direct war action against the locks and the River is now in prospect." At a board of directors meeting on 15 January, Wood was instructed to direct the LCA concerns to Secretary of War Henry Stimson; and his letter of 19 January requested that Stimson "review measures which have been taken to protect the canal against possible sabotage or attack."[11]

Instead of dealing directly with the LCA request, Stimson referred the letter to the War Department, resulting in a response that infuriated Wood. In a letter dated 28 January 1942, Major General E. S. Adams acknowledged receipt of the LCA resolution requesting protection for the locks and then stated that "the policy of the War Department in such matters is that the protection of life and property is a primary responsibility of the local and state governments concerned" and that the use of federal troops would be contemplated only when "the protection afforded by the responsible agencies . . . is deemed inadequate." In conclusion, Adams informed Wood that the resolution would be forwarded back to Sixth Corps Area for consideration. Up to this point, the LCA had been working "within channels" in its efforts to obtain some assurance from the military that the importance of adequate protection for the locks was recognized; but it was becoming apparent that the military was not about to discuss security details with civilians, no matter how directly concerned they might be with the subject matter.[12]

Immediately upon receipt of the Adams letter, an attorney representing the LCA fired off a letter to Michigan senator Prentiss M. Brown, calling the army's response "inane and meaningless" and advising that "the War Department should not expect [thereby]to gain the confidence of the public or the people in the lake industry, with respect to the protection of such a vital point in the transportation of our raw materials." Another vague communication from Major General J. M. Cummins of the Sixth Corps Area, assuring that "all measures necessary" were being taken to safeguard the locks did nothing to clarify the situation; and on 27 February, Wood played what was probably his final card, eliciting the aid of the new ODT boss, Joseph Eastman. In his letter of that date, Wood traced the details of his ten-week effort to obtain military assurance of adequate protective measures and informed Eastman that he had been "literally besieged with inquiries from officials of vessel and steel companies," including a phone call on 26 February from the chairman of the board of the U.S. Steel Company, all wanting to know the details of the defense measures taken. Wood acknowledged that it might not be wise for the military to make the specific measures taken known to all but urged that it would be appropriate to "inform some civilian having direct interest in lake transportation so that he may assure others in this regard, without necessarily informing them concerning the nature of the protective facilities." In closing, Wood indicated to Eastman, "[You] could with propriety request the War Department to advise you in detail concerning the measures which are now in effect or have been authorized to safeguard the canal," and, "[If you] and other appropriate executives of ODT, including myself, were satisfied that the action taken by the War Department is sufficient, we would then be in a position to quiet the prevailing uneasiness relative to the vulnerability of the canal."[13]

Eastman immediately followed up Wood's request with a letter to the War Department that finally broke through the bureaucratic logjam. On 5 March 1942, Eastman received a War Department response indicating that "the Chief of Staff personally has expressed a keen interest in the protection of this key to the lake transportation system" and that "measures would soon be taken to increase the defenses from both ground and air and to make sabotage by means of blocking the channel much more difficult." While the War Department "naturally hesitates to publish the exact measures taken," Eastman was asked to reassure the Great Lakes shipping industry that the defense of the locks was now a top priority; and Wood was able to inform Pittsburgh Steamship Company president A. H. Ferbert, "Based on information which I received in Washington, there is a great deal more concern relative to protection of the St. Marys Falls Canal than heretofore."[14]

The War Department had long recognized the strategic significance of the locks; but in the aftermath of Pearl Harbor, there was no clear military consensus as to the capabilities of the Axis to launch an assault against this target, without which there could be no agreement as to the extent of defensive measures necessary. An internal Naval Department memorandum of 19 January advocated that "a ground force of not less than ten thousand (10,000) be deployed strategically, equipped with automatics, machine guns and rifles," while a War Department assessment claimed that "the equivalent of an Army Corps will be required" to provide an effective defense "commensurate with the importance of the objective." Military decision makers were understandably reluctant to detail such an enormous number of troops to the protection of an internal facility at a time when their resources were thinly stretched around the globe. In early February, General Marshall ordered that the military police battalion on guard at the Soo be reinforced by a detachment of the 100th Coast Artillery and a barrage-balloon battery; additionally, the chiefs of Infantry, Air Forces, and Engineers were to prepare systematic evaluations of the extent of the Axis threat and the forces reasonably necessary to protect against that threat.[15]

The evaluations prepared in response to this order credited the Germans

63

with the ability to launch several different types of attack against the Soo facilities, including long-range bombing, torpedo-plane and dive bombing. While each of these methods was within the realm of possibility, each involved extraordinary difficulties in planning and execution. The Sault Ste. Marie region was some thirty-five hundred miles from Axis-held territory in northern Europe, within one-way flying range of the German HE-177 high-altitude bomber; but an assault of this nature had little likelihood of success, since the locks offered too small a target for high-altitude bombing. A much greater risk was posed by a combination of dive bombers and torpedo planes, but these aircraft had limited range and could not reach the target from Europe. The concern, however, was that the Germans would send ships into the far reaches of the Hudson Bay region and attempt to mount an attack with torpedo planes from these remote locations, which were within flying range of the Soo. From the Axis viewpoint, such an action posed major problems of coordination and—perhaps more importantly—could not be launched until mid-to-late summer, when the ice finally released its grip in the far north. The military regarded this last point as crucial, since disruption of the locks would be most critical in the spring, when iron ore stockpiles at the lower lake ports had been depleted.[16]

The third type of assault (and the one most feared by the War Department planners) was attack by German paratroopers. Under this scenario, assault troops would be delivered to the target in one of several types of German seaplanes capable of flying the great distances involved. After landing in one of several acceptable sites on the outskirts of the American Soo, the troops would form up and attack the locks, quickly overwhelming the military police battalion, which was not trained or equipped to meet such an assault. Once the locks were in enemy hands, army engineers reported that a force of one hundred demolition experts with four tons of high explosives could completely destroy the gates and operating machinery of all three operational locks in just half an hour. Following such damage (the engineers went on to estimate), it would take four months to bring one lock back into operation and a full year before all three could be utilized.[17]

While military planners recognized that a direct attack against the locks at the Soo was very unlikely (Brigadier General Dwight D. Eisenhower's opinion was that "any attack against them must take the form of a military adventure rather than of a methodical approach"), the catastrophic results of a successful enemy operation were such that the War Department moved immediately to strengthen the defensive force assigned. In March, the Sault Ste. Marie Military District was formed under the authority of the Central Defense Command in Memphis, Tennessee, thus placing the entire Sault Ste. Marie area under direct military control; and on 28 March, the 131st Infantry Regiment replaced the 702nd Military Police Battalion. During the following months, additional antiaircraft and barrage-balloon elements were added to the defense forces, as well as two companies of chemical-warfare troops to provide smoke defense. At peak levels, a force in excess of seven thousand troops was defending the locks, and the area was referred to as "probably the most heavily defended in the country." One individual described a 1942 passage through the locks aboard the passenger ship *South American*:

> The Soo locks were carefully guarded by American and Canadian soldiers, complete with machine gun nests, anti-aircraft guns and barrage balloons. No visitors were permitted at the locks so the only way one could observe them was to be aboard a vessel actually locking through. The only sad part of the trip from my standpoint was the ruling that no cameras could be permitted on deck while in port, passing through the Soo or cruising in the channels of the St. Mary's river and the St. Clair river.[18]

The quartering of seven thousand troops in a town with a civilian population of fifteen thousand was not without difficulty. Army engineers and construction crews worked to provide temporary shelter for the men and equipment, and the troops were belatedly supplied with arctic clothing to protect them from the harsh climate.[19]

One of the most fascinating social experiments of the wartime years on the lakes began in early March 1942, when advance elements of the 100th Coast Artillery—a "colored" unit in the terminology of the segregated army of World War II—began arriving at the Soo. This regiment, consisting of some eighteen hundred draftees clustered around a cadre of 168 enlisted men, had been activated in March 1941 at Camp Davis, North Carolina, and was assigned to the Soo to provide antiaircraft protection for the locks. Prior to the arrival of this unit, there had been only two African–American families residing in the Sault Ste. Marie area; the sudden appearance of several thousand young black men caused some apprehension among the civilian population. Shortly after the arrival of the troops, N. C. Casey—director of the local United Services Organization (USO) office and an African-American himself—sought to allay some of these fears when he addressed the local Kiwanis Club. According to the Soo *Evening News*, Mr. Casey told the assembly, "I realize to the fullest the shock which many citizens here got from the shipment here of hundreds of Negro soldiers; [however,] you and your women folks may go to sleep each night confident that our boys will not violate your confidence in them as honorable soldiers of the U.S.A. and good American citizens."[20]

While many Sault Ste. Marie civilians may have been "shocked" by the presence of the blacks, the same could well be said for the young soldiers, many of whom were natives of the deep South, totally unaccustomed to the harsh winter weather of Michigan's Upper Peninsula. One of the most immediate and pressing problems posed was the complete lack of recreational opportunities for these troops. The Detroit chapter of the National Association for the Advancement of Colored People sought to fill this gap by arranging a series of dances for the soldiers. Several busloads of young black women traveled up from Detroit "under strict chaperons" for the weekend festivities. Following the dances, they spent the night on army cots at the USO site, with armed military guards at the door, before returning to Detroit the next day. In July 1942, Major W. F. Train reported to Washington on some of the social difficulties being experienced by the men of the 100th Coast Artillery in a memorandum sated with the discrimination inherent in the army of his day:

> The Society for the Advancement of the Colored Race [sic] conducts a group of Negro women under strict chaperons from the Detroit area to the "Soo" about once a month for dancing. This bright spot in the drab routine is about the only recreation available. However, the Italian quarter of the Canadian "Soo" has accepted the 100th Coast Artillery as southern Indians. This impression has been recently corrected, and the Canadians are making efforts to eliminate the conviviality originally established. The 100th Coast Artillery has also been accepted by an Indian colony in the vicinity. Since this condition exists and since the Negro is not well adapted to the rigorous climate, it is believed that the 100th Coast Artillery should be moved from this area before winter.[21]

As was true at military bases across the country, the presence of large numbers of young men in the community caused a significant increase in local crime. In August 1942, two black soldiers were charged by military authorities with the rape of a fourteen-year-old Sault Ste. Marie girl. After noting that the military penalty for this offense was death, the *Evening News* editorialized: "Law and order demand that the men guilty in this case be punished to the extent of the law. We have confidence that there will be quick justice." By December, the men had been convicted of the charges but no penalty had been announced, causing the paper to ask, "How much longer will we need to wait to know that they have been properly punished for the heinous crime committed?" Following this editorial, the Chippewa County prosecutor requested that the two soldiers be returned to Michigan for punishment; but the army announced on 21 December that the defendants had been sentenced to life in prison to be served in Fort Leavenworth, Kansas.[22]

While problems were inevitable, it appears that the presence of the 100th Coast Artillery was essentially a positive experience for both the soldiers and the people of the Soo area. In 1942, there existed genuine concern that an attack upon the locks was imminent, so the civilians genuinely appreciated the protection afforded by the troops of the 100th Coast Artillery, as well as those of the other units in the area. A full-page advertisement in the *Evening News* on 6 April 1942, sponsored by many local merchants, was headlined: WELCOME BUDDIES! SAULT STE. MARIE IS PROUD OF YOU and went on to say:

> We invite you to participate with us in all the affairs of our community life, on the basis of friendly comradeship. You are most cordially urged to get acquainted with us; to attend our churches, our theatres; to eat in our restaurants; to visit and trade in our fine stores. THANKS YANKS! In the shelter of your anti-aircraft guns and of your barrage balloons, searchlights and listening devices, and in the knowledge that you are several thousand of Uncle Sam's best defenders, we feel secure against any alien enemy. We are your friends, as you are ours.

Looking back on those times, Milton Ward, a veteran of the 100th Coast Artillery recalls the people of the Soo area as "grand": "We didn't have any problem there, we went any where we wanted. We really didn't have any problem, no discrimination." He is particularly proud of the fact that his son was the first Afro–American child born at the Soo's War Memorial Hospital. Another veteran of the unit, a native of New Orleans, described his tour at the Soo as "pretty smooth," with the exception of the winter weather, to which he was never able to adjust.[23]

In addition to the military personnel, the Sault Ste. Marie area also received an influx of construction workers who were building the new Mac-Arthur Lock (see chapter 6); and the combination of the two groups caused acute shortages throughout the first eighteen months of the war effort. In May 1942, the Office of Price Administration (OPA) declared Chippewa County a "defense rental area," requiring landlords to roll back rental rates to those in effect on 1 March, while the *Evening News* in an October editorial asked all property owners to consider taking in borders to address the "serious problem" of housing shortages. The same paper reported that local restaurants were so overwhelmed with customers that many were forced to close their doors for lack of food and help.[24]

In addition to housing shortages and crime problems, the military presence was also disruptive in other, less significant ways: the records of the units involved are replete with references to runaway barrage balloons and smoke obscuration tests gone awry. The balloons were particularly trouble-some, since they had a tendency to break loose from their moorings in high winds and once free, their trailing cables would do significant damage to electrical and telephone lines. After several such incidents, the army worked out an agreement with the Edison Company to have all current shut off im-mediately upon notice of an escaped balloon, to minimize the possibility of fires. Once loose, the balloons would travel great distances, with newspaper articles reporting damage as far south as Saginaw, Michigan and as far east as Ottawa, Canada.[25]

While the defenses arrayed at the Soo were extensive, one important ele-ment repeatedly recommended was never supplied for the defense of the locks. In a War Department memo of 6 March 1942, the chief of staff was advised "that one squadron of interceptor aviation and appropriate detector devises [should] be located within the Sault Ste. Marie Military District, effective May 1, 1942." Given the nature of the threats to the Soo, fighter de-fense was certainly appropriate. But the military was desperately short of trained pursuit squadrons and, although three landing fields were prepared, the decision was made to delay provision of fighter protection until "sometime during 1943." Similar supply and priority problems existed with respect to long-range radar, and the forces protecting the locks were forced to make due with short-range sets.[26]

All of the attack scenarios considered by the War Department featured enemy aircraft approaching from the north. For this reason, officers aboard the lake freighter were urged to keep a sharp eye out for unusual aircraft con-centrations over Lake Superior. During the winter of 1942–43, the military provided a one-day seminar for some of these men on aircraft identification, including techniques for estimating course and speed. Fortunately, none of these men were ever called on to utilize these skills; but one officer did report sighting one of the incendiary balloons released in Japan that caused spo-radic injuries and damage, mostly in the Pacific Northwest.[27]

By the spring of 1943, several factors caused the War Department to reevaluate the need for significant defense forces at the Soo. While the Ger-man Luftwaffe was probably just as capable of launching an assault as they had been a year earlier, the aura of invincibility that had surrounded the Nazi forces had been shattered by their staggering losses at Stalingrad and El Alamein. Additionally, the psychological hangover of the Pearl Harbor at-tack had begun to fade, and experience had provided American military planners with a better appreciation of the extraordinary technical difficulties posed by the type of suicide attack necessary to destroy the locks. The addi-tion of the soon-to-be-completed MacArthur Lock (see chapter 6), plus the nearby storage of newly fabricated replacement gates and other spare parts, served to make the facility that much less vulnerable and a long-term shut down much less likely. On 25 May 1943, the War Department slashed the defense forces to a total of two thousand troops consisting of one infantry battalion, one antiaircraft battalion, and one company of air-raid warning personnel. In December 1943, all of these units were removed, as well, and a single battalion of military police were again guarding the locks—the same-size force that had been in place prior to the 1942 buildup.[28]

While the Soo locks were certainly the most vital and vulnerable of potential targets, steps were taken to protect other Great Lakes facilities, as well. In late December 1941, the chief executive officer of each of the companies engaged in transporting iron ore received a visit from an agent of the Federal Bureau of Investigation, hand-delivering a copy of an eight-page epistle on industry security matters written by bureau director J. Edgar Hoover and addressed to President Wood of the LCA. Hoover revealed that an "extensive survey" of Great Lakes facilities had recently been completed by his agents and, after reminding Wood that primary responsibility for the protection of the industry was with the individual fleetowners, detailed numerous "suggestions" that might aid them in discharging this responsibility. The FBI boss acknowledged the existence of the rules previously adopted by the LCA in August of 1940 and advised that his suggestions were "not intended to take the place of [these] resolutions, but rather they should be regarded as complimentary thereto."[29]

Among the measures proposed by Hoover were a standardized industry employment application form, background investigations, fingerprinting, exclusion of passengers and visitors from vessels, and the posting of engine rooms as restricted areas. In addition, he requested that the prior LCA rules be more strictly enforced, particularly with respect to screening and searching those coming aboard the boats and searching the vessels before entry into the Soo locks. Hoover also stated his desire that security measures of the industry be "coordinated and standardized" and his belief that the LCA was "in a position to disseminate information and formulate plans which may bring this about." On 15 January 1942, the LCA reaffirmed its previous resolution of 1 August 1940, added the suggestions made by Hoover, and subsequently circulated to all association members a booklet entitled *Rules for the Protection of Great Lakes Commerce During the Present War*. The rules set forth in this booklet remained the basic security measures of the industry throughout the war years.[30]

In addition to the security efforts of the LCA and its individual members, the U.S. Coast Guard exercised considerable authority over various aspects of the Great Lakes shipping industry through its Captain of the Port (COTP)

69

program, which placed a Coast Guard officer in charge of security issues at each of twenty-nine key ports across the country. In the Great Lakes area, COTPs were designated for Sault Ste. Marie, Cleveland, Detroit, Chicago, and Duluth. These offices were empowered, under the terms of Executive Order No. 8972, to place armed guards upon any waterfront installations they deemed to be essential for national defense. This authority was later augmented with Executive Order No. 9074, issued on 25 February 1942, which provided that the COTPs could take all steps or issue any regulations or orders for safeguarding domestic shipping.[31]

In order to discharge this heavy responsibility, the Coast Guard was forced to rely, in large measure, upon the efforts of Temporary Reservists, civilians who served on a part-time, unpaid basis, contributing a minimum of twelve hours of service each week. These individuals, who averaged over forty years of age, underwent difficult training and had the same authority as full-time, paid Coast Guard Reserve members. Most of them held full-time jobs in the civilian economy and "a boat crew or a dock watch made up of such men as a grocer, a business executive, an automobile mechanic, a school teacher, a pressman, and an apartment house janitor was entirely typical." Their contributions to the war effort included guarding ships, bridges, wharfs, and other shoreline installations, as well as manning small craft that patrolled harbors and rivers. Some fifty thousand individuals served as "TRs" (as they were called), freeing an estimated eighty-two hundred regular guardsmen for sea duty.[32]

Temporary Reserves also played a direct role in guarding ore freighters during the later war years. On 24 July 1942, Ninth Naval District officials ordered the Coast Guard in Cleveland and Chicago to assign two-to-four armed enlisted men to each American-flag vessel that regularly transited the Soo Locks, resulting in an additional drain on regular Coast Guard personnel. The initial purpose for the guards was only to prevent any sabotage efforts at the locks; however, the decision was made to leave the guards on board for the entire trip, so as to avoid the necessity of stopping the ship to pick them up and drop them off. The number of men assigned to each ship depended upon the accommodations available; most of the older lake ships had been built in the days when the boats were manned by only two six-hour watches, so what little extra space was available had long since been used for extra sleeping room for the men of the newly added third watch.[33]

The presence of these armed men aboard the freighters was unlike anything seen before (or since) on the lakes, and relationships between crew and guard were sometimes difficult. Most of the coastguardsmen were young, enlisted personnel fresh from basic training ("They were just kids!," said one lake captain); and they served aboard the ships without direct supervision, since it was simply not possible to place officers aboard each boat. During the early months of the program, there were occasional confrontations between the perhaps overly zealous young guards and the civilian officers of the ship and it was clear that lines of authority had to be clarified. In October 1942, all of the officers aboard the lake freighters were commissioned as Temporary Reserve officers in the Coast Guard, thus providing them with direct and clear authority over the enlisted guards aboard their ships. During the manpower crunch of the later war years, all of the regular Coast Guard personnel were removed from the boats, while the commissioning of the regular ship officers as Temporary Reservists allowed for a continued military presence.

Loaded weapons and inexperienced personnel were a combination that may well have posed a greater danger to the crews of the lake boats than did anything seriously considered in Berlin. The *Detroit News* reported on 13 July 1942 that a newly arrived engineer was shot by a guard aboard the supply ship *Frontier* when the guard "not recognizing the stranger on board and failing to get satisfaction from him, fired." The captain of one ship in the Columbia fleet simply confiscated all of the ammunition aboard his boat and kept it under lock and key in his office, forcing the coastguardsmen to patrol the vessel with empty weapons. While providing "security," the enlisted personnel were also supposed to receive additional training in seamanship from the crew of the laker; but it appears that for the most part, they simply went for an extended boat ride. One laker remembered, "All they did was eat!"[34]

While most lake officers regarded the armed guard program as a nuisance, they did enjoy the "benefits" of being commissioned officers in the Coast Guard—most importantly, the uniforms issued to them when they were sworn in, which included everything from dress whites to raincoats, overcoats, and even shoes, which were rationed for the civilian population. While uniforms had never been worn aboard lake freighters in peacetime, many a sailor would don his new apparel at the slightest opportunity and strut about as "an officer and a gentleman." The uniforms were particularly effective ashore, where officer raiment could secure a seat on a crowded bus or train or admit one to a movie theater free of charge. These pursuits were not, however, without some risk. With his ship unloading ore in Buffalo harbor, Clarence McTevia donned his new ensign uniform for a trip to the downtown post office. As he strutted proudly through the door, he came face to face with a "real" Coast Guard officer "covered with brass" and carrying a "dignity whip." McTevia "snapped" to attention and delivered a feeble imitation of a salute that invoked only a glare, all the while "shivering in his boots." Upon his return to the ship, he ordered one of the enlisted coast guardsmen to his room for an extensive training lesson in the military art of a correct salute.[35]

Among the principal concerns of the Coast Guard was the security of the narrow channels of the St. Marys, St. Clair, and Detroit Rivers, where the sinking of a freighter in the shipping lanes could shut off the flow of iron ore like a cork in a bottle. This threat was recognized at the highest level when the issue of constructing an alternative route to bypass the Soo Locks was discussed at the WPB meeting of 4 August 1942 (see chapter 5). When William S. Knudsen remarked that "the sinking of a boat in the St. Claire [sic] River would cause almost as great difficulties as damage to the locks," he was assured that "precautions were taken against such contingencies." The nature of these precautions had been a matter of some controversy in the Great Lakes region during the spring of 1942. In April, the Coast Guard announced a requirement that anyone who owned or operated any kind of private vessel (ncluding even a rowboat or canoe) had to obtain—and display upon request—an identification card issued by the Coast Guard. While only the person in charge of the particular boat was required to have the card, that person had to be able to vouch for any other occupant of the vessel. The next month, the Coast Guard announced another policy that would have all but eliminated recreational boating and fishing on the connecting waters of the Great Lakes. Under this new ruling, no vessels under one hundred feet in length could be operated on the Detroit, St. Clair, St. Marys, or Rouge Rivers or Lake St. Clair unless a permit was obtained from a Coast Guard office at least seven days in advance of the proposed trip. In order to obtain this permit, a holder of a Coast Guard identification card would have to include details of the exact course to be followed by the boat on its proposed outing.[36]

The obvious intent of the Coast Guard in promulgating these rules was to eliminate the danger of a tiny fishing vessel loaded with explosives being rammed into the side of a freighter in these narrow, crowded channels. The net effect, however, would be virtually to eliminate recreational use of these waterways, most of which were readily accessible from the metropolitan Detroit area and represented one of the few attractive diversions available to war workers. While the proposed restrictions may have been otherwise warranted by the danger to wartime transportation, this cost was adjudged to be too high, and "the roar of disapproval that arose from the boating and fishing fraternity in the Detroit area" soon brought about significant modifications, including the elimination of the advance-permit requirement. The new "interpretation" of the restrictions required that all boats that were self-propelled or in excess of sixteen feet in length be registered with the Coast Guard and have the registration numbers displayed. No pleasure craft was allowed to cross a ship channel in the hours from sunset to sunrise, and a vessel crossing a ship channel during daylight hours was required to remain at a stated distance from freighter traffic. All such boats were also to remain at least three hundred feet away from any dock, plant, or installation that was "directly or indirectly" connected with the war effort. This last provision was so ambiguous that fishermen were simply advised to avoid any commercial building and also to remain at least five hundred feet away from shipping channels. The use of cameras was also prohibited, whether from boats or along the shoreline. All of these restrictions were strictly enforced by the Coast Guard Temporary Reserves, who regularly patrolled the connecting waterways in small craft; and violators were subject to penalties ranging as high as ten years' imprisonment and fines of up to ten thousand dollars.[37]

One further security issue that involved a significant departure from "business as usual" in the shipping industry dealt with the traditional publication of "vessel passages" and "port lists" in newspapers around the Great Lakes region. The vessel passages provided the names of individual ships and the times at which they passed specific points on the lakes, such as the Soo Locks, the Straits of Mackinac, and the Detroit River, while the port lists provided the names of ships entering or departing from specific ports, as well as information on the nature of the cargos carried. Relatives and friends were able to keep track of Great Lakes sailors by following ship movements in their local papers. Immediately after the attack on Pearl Harbor, the U.S. Maritime Commission "requested" that newspapers discontinue any reporting on ship movements; newspapers around the Great Lakes region quickly complied. A short time later, the U.S. Office of Censorship, in keeping with its wartime policy of voluntary censorship, issued a code to the newspaper industry naming eight specified topics that papers were to avoid in their reporting, one of which included "location, movements, and identity of American and Allied naval and merchant ships." On 10 March 1942, the Office of Censorship went one step further, issuing an order specifically prohibiting the publication of Great Lakes shipping information.[38]

The LCA greatly favored the continued publication of vessel passage information as a service to its members. A. T. Wood wrote to Rear Admiral H. L. Vickery of the Maritime Commission on 17 March, urging a reconsideration of the decision. Wood pointed out in this communication that continued publication would pose little danger to the industry, particularly in light of the fact that the Canadian government had reached a contrary conclusion, allowing the papers of that nation to continue publishing vessel passages and port lists. Wood also prevailed upon Congressman Fred Bradley, of the Michigan limestone port of Rogers City, to take the matter up with the Office of Censorship; and these efforts proved successful when he was informed by Vickery on 31 March that "the normal publication of ship movements in the ore, coal, grain, merchandise, and passenger traffic restricted to the Great Lakes does not violate the regulations of the Code of War Time Practices for the American Press." Wood immediately forwarded this good news on to the press but was unpleasantly surprised by the unenthusiastic response. Editor Paul Bellamy of the *Cleveland Plain Dealer* informed Wood that despite the reconsideration by the Office of Censorship, his paper would not resume printing vessel passage and port lists due to the "considerable expense" and the necessity for the paper to save money in this "year of rising costs." After all, said Bellamy, "a war costs a newspaper money. It is not a defense industry, which profits at that time." It seems that much of the newspaper industry in the Great Lakes region welcomed the opportunity to stop running the routine shipping items, since most vessel passages and port lists were not resumed until late in the war.[39]*

During the war years, not a single incident of sabotage was reported on the Great Lakes. However, this fact may be more correctly attributed to a lack of effort on the part of the nation's enemies than to the security measures actually taken by government and industry. Richard Gid Powers reports in his work *Secrecy and Power: The Life of J. Edgar Hoover* that out of 19,649 investigated reports, not a single act of enemy agent sabotage was ever proven to have occurred in the United States during World War II; it appears that neither Germany nor Japan mounted any serious sabotage efforts. This fact makes it difficult to evaluate the success of the steps actually taken to defend the industry; however, considering the importance of the iron ore shipments to the war effort, these measures were certainly necessary and prudent. The entire security program also demonstrates, again, the cooperative relationship that existed between the Great Lakes shipping industry and the federal government throughout these years. The industry cooperated completely with the Coast Guard Captain of the Port program and was instrumental in focusing military attention on the importance of the Soo Locks and in helping to free hundreds of coastguardsmen for service overseas by providing guards for the ships and installations. Most importantly, the industry, acting through the offices of the LCA, initiated its own security measures, which remained the foundation of the basic security program until 1945.[40]

For the men who worked on the freighters during these years, the security programs are highlights that link their toils with the larger war effort. Coast

---

*The Newspaper Scrapbook Collection at the Institute for Great Lakes Research contains less than half the volume of clippings for the years 1942–45 than for those years immediately before and after, while most of the vessel passages and port lists included are from Canadian newspapers.

Guard uniforms, armed guards, barrage balloons, and machine-gun em-placements all underscored the importance of the job they did in providing the raw materials necessary for the nation's production performance.

The 631-foot *Harry Coulby* of the Interlake Steamship Company, the largest freighter on the lakes on the eve of World War II. Photo courtesy of the Institute for Great Lakes Research, Bowling Green State University.

Iron ore loading docks at Superior, Wisconsin. Photo courtesy of the Institute for Great Lakes Research, Bowling Green State University.

Loading chutes on iron ore loading dock at Duluth, Minnesota. Photo courtesy of the Institute for Great Lakes Research, Bowling Green State University.

Hulett unloader at work on a bulk carrier. Photo courtesy of the Institute for Great
Lakes Research, Bowling Green State University.

The bulk freighter *Anna C. Minch*, lost on Lake Michigan in the Armistice Day Storm of 1940. Photo courtesy of the Institute for Great Lakes Research, Bowling Green State University.

The *George W. Perkins*, on which Edward Baganz had his wild ride during the Armistice Day Storm. Photo courtesy of the Institute for Great Lakes Research, Bowling Green State University.

Partially collapsed railroad bridge blocking the downbound approach to the Davis and Sabin Locks, Sault Ste. Marie, 7 October 1941. Photo courtesy of the Institute for Great Lakes Research, Bowling Green State University.

Aerial view of the Defoe Shipbuilding Company, Bay City, Michigan. Defoe received a contract for the construction of twenty-eight of these 307-foot destroyer escorts. Photo courtesy of the Institute for Great Lakes Research, Bowling Green State University.

The Leathem D. Smith Shipbuilding Company, Sturgeon Bay, Wisconsin, 1944.
Photo courtesy of the Institute for Great Lakes Research, Bowling Green State
University.

Two 258-foot cargo vessels under construction for the Maritime Commission at the
Leathem D. Smith yard, 1943. Photo courtesy of the Institute for Great Lakes
Research, Bowling Green State University.

Prefabricated bow section of a 173-foot subchaser at the Leathem D. Smith Company, 1944. Photo courtesy of the Institute for Great Lakes Research, Bowling Green State University.

Mrs. Oliva Dionne and her famous quintuplets shortly after their arrival in Superior, Wisconsin for the launching of five cargo vessels, 9 May 1943. AP/Wide World Photos.

John LeCorn's *Tampico*. Photo courtesy of the Institute for Great Lakes Research, Bowling Green State University.

U.S. Army troops guarding the new MacArthur Lock at the Soo, 12 July 1943. Note the barrage balloon flying above the freighter in the background. AP/Wide World Photos.

A barrage balloon of the 399th Barrage Balloon Battalion at Fort Brady, Sault Ste. Marie, circa 1942. Marquette County Historical Society.

The palatial passenger liner *Seeandbee* at the East Ninth Street Pier, Cleveland, circa 1939. Photo courtesy of the Institute for Great Lakes Research, Bowling Green State University.

The *Seeandbee* under guard and being stripped of furnishings following requisition by the U.S. Navy for conversion to an aircraft carrier, 1942. Photo courtesy of the Institute for Great Lakes Research, Bowling Green State University.

The USS *Wolverine*. Photo courtesy of the Institute for Great Lakes Research, Bowling Green State University.

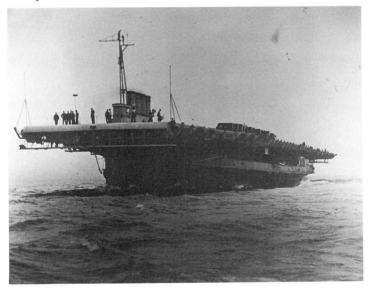

The steamer *George M. Humphrey* being raised from the bottom of the Straits of Mackinac, 1944. Photo courtesy of the Institute for Great Lakes Research, Bowling Green State University.

Forward end of the *George M. Humphrey* following raising. Photo courtesy of the Institute for Great Lakes Research, Bowling Green State University.

The U.S. Coast Guard Cutter *Mackinaw* leading three new seagoing transports through the ice-choked St. Marys River, January, 1945. Photo courtesy of the Institute for Great Lakes Research, Bowling Green State University.

The *Leon Fraser*, one of five new bulk freighters built for the Pittsburgh Steamship Company in 1941–42. Photo courtesy of the Institute for Great Lakes Research, Bowling Green State University.

The launching of the *Thomas Wilson*, the first of the Maritime Class freighters. Photo courtesy of the Institute for Great Lakes Research, Bowling Green State University.

The Maritime Class freighter *Champlain*, originally the *Belle Isle*. Photo courtesy of the Institute for Great Lakes Research, Bowling Green State University.

The launching of the *Belle Isle*, 15 November 1943. Photo courtesy of the Institute for Great Lakes Research, Bowling Green State University.

The first aerial photograph of the Soo Locks taken after wartime restrictions were lifted, 26 March 1946. The new MacArthur Lock is at the far right. Photo courtesy of the Institute for Great Lakes Research, Bowling Green State University.

5
The Manpower Crisis

WANTED—Registered druggist; young or old, deaf or dumb. Must have license and walk without crutches. Apply Cloverleaf Drug Store.
—Classified Advertisement, 1942

Manpower! For ten years the Roosevelt administration had struggled to find jobs for workers; now it had to find workers for jobs.
—James MacGregor Burns

With an average crew of forty men, the ships of the Great Lakes iron ore fleet required some twelve thousand sailors to man the bulk carriers, while several thousand more were needed for the self-unloaders, package freighters, car ferries, and passenger ships. While this total might seem a relatively small number when considering the significance of the task, manpower shortages posed one of the most difficult problems to face Great Lakes shippers during the war years. The solid manpower core of officers and experienced sailors working their way up the ranks provided the industry with a measure of stability, but a large percentage of those employed on the boats were single young men attracted by the relatively high pay and the nomadic existence of the job. This latter group was particularly vulnerable to the draft; but large numbers of men also left the lakes during the war years to meet the great demand for ocean sailors, while others abandoned the boats for the plentiful, high-paying jobs in the defense industry ashore.

The particular susceptibility of the industry employment situation to national and international events was demonstrated by fluctuations in the job market during the 1939, 1940, and 1941 seasons. The outbreak of war in Europe triggered a shipping boom in the fall of 1939 that brought virtually full employment to the lakes, and thousands of Depression-weary sailors were available to fill the positions. While the war brought about increased demand for seamen, it also brought about intense competition for these jobs from another source. The submarine war in the Atlantic caused "another horde of ocean-going salts" to head for the Great Lakes in the spring of 1940, where a sailor could earn comparable pay without the danger present on the oceans; as a result, no manpower shortages existed on the lakes prior to the 1941 season.[1]

On 16 September 1940, President Roosevelt signed into law the Selective Training and Service Act of 1940, which required the registration of all American men in the twenty-one-to-thirty-five age group on 16 October 1940. In order to accomplish this objective with a minimum of disruption to lake shipments, the LCA prevailed upon the government to set up thirty-eight special registration offices in twenty-nine of the principal loading and unloading ports around the lakes, with the result that 4,243 sailors were registered without having to leave their employment to do so. The act established some fifty-five hundred local civilian draft boards, each of which had the authority to grant an industrial deferment to an individual "if it was determined that his most useful contribution to the Nation's welfare was in his civilian activity and occupation." While the national offices of the Selective Service System provided the local boards with standards to follow, the final decision to grant a deferment was left to the local board on a case-by-case basis.[2]

The passage of the Selective Training and Service Act had a significant effect in contributing to a shortage of Great Lakes sailors during the 1941 season. On 15 March 1941, the Selective Service System issued Memorandum I-23 to all state directors, urging serious deferment consideration for merchant seamen, with the result that many of the sailors who had flocked to the lakes during the 1940 season chose to return to the ocean, where deferments were available. Voluntary enlistments also took their toll on the numbers of Great Lakes sailors available, since many chose to enlist in the service branch of their choice, rather than await the draft call; and a port-by-port recruitment effort by the navy was particularly effective during the winter of 1940/41. On 23 May 1941, as a result of efforts by the LCA, the Selective Service System issued its Memorandum I-117 to all state directors, extending "special occupational deferment consideration to seamen on the Great Lakes and in inland waterways shipping"; and the manpower situation stabilized on the lakes for the 1941 season.[3]

The extended winter lay-up of lake vessels caused the industry a peculiar problem with the local draft boards, which often considered sailors home for the winter as available for immediate induction. The LCA convened a meeting with representatives of several governmental agencies in Cleveland on 5 December 1941 to devise an acceptable program with the result that lake seamen were referred to local offices of the U.S. Employment Service

(USES) at season's end, where temporary employment was obtained for the winter months. This arrangement was acceptable to most of the local boards, and it was also agreed to grant continued deferments to men attending winter classes to qualify as licensed officers. The LCA also distributed three thousand copies of a booklet entitled *Manning of Great Lakes Vessels as Affected by Selective Training and Service Act* to hundreds of local draft boards throughout the Midwest in an effort to educate draft board members on the scope and significance of the Great Lakes shipping industry.[4]

These LCA efforts worked fairly well to secure an adequate pool of personnel during the 1942 season; but by 1943, occasional shortages and problems began to occur. On 8 June 1943, the *Toledo Blade* reported an accusation from an official of the Maritime Union that local draft boards in the Toledo area were calling up sailors who were temporarily unemployed between ship assignments, with the result that ships were leaving Toledo harbor with serious crew deficiencies and "one ship left with such a small crew that the men had to be assigned to 16 hour shifts." Selective Service officials denied the allegations and contended that any such problems actually resulted from failure of employers to file necessary paperwork with the draft boards; but the same officials did acknowledge that local boards were being forced to draft single men and married men without children, regardless of employment, in order to avoid drafting fathers.[5]

The 1943 manpower shortage came to a head during the month of August, with the War Department actually giving consideration to the use of Italian prisoners of war aboard the lake freighters. This suggestion was quickly scuttled because of the obvious danger of sabotage but also because of an opinion from the Office of the Judge Advocate General that service aboard a lake freighter was a "hazardous occupation" as defined by the Geneva Convention, thus prohibiting such employment for prisoners of war. Even without the use of these prisoners, the personnel shortages were overcome following a series of meetings in Washington at which it was agreed that the Recruiting and Manpower Office (RMO) of the War Shipping Administration would discontinue recruitment for saltwater sailors in the states surrounding the Great Lakes and that Selective Service director Lewis B. Hershey would telegraph draft board directors around the Great Lakes, reemphasizing the importance of the industry to the war effort and requesting that they "consider seriously" the deferment of sailors whenever possible.[6]

The deferment problems experienced by the Great Lakes shipping industry during the 1943 season were a mere preview of the manpower crisis that would afflict the industry—and the entire nation—during 1944. The growth of the American armed forces had been gradual during the early months of the war, because there were simply not enough training facilities, instructors, clothing, or weapons immediately available to train and equip the vast numbers that would eventually be needed. But by the end of 1943, these problems had been solved, the armed forces had reached a strength of 7,500,000 men and were demanding that local draft boards supply even more. The War Department was also alarmed at the rising average age of the soldiers, which had reached twenty-five by the end of 1943, but since all available draftees in the under-twenty-six age group had already been taken, the only remaining available source of young recruits was the pool of those who had received industrial and agricultural deferments. On 26 February 1944, General George Marshall, chief of staff of the army, drafted a memorandum for the signature of the president, which was then sent to all of the local draft boards around the country, advising that "the Nation's manpower pool has been dangerously depleted by liberal deferments and I am convinced that in this respect we have been overly lenient, particularly with regard to younger men." The president closed his message with a request that the local boards review all occupational deferments in an effort to release more of the younger men for the armed forces.[7]

The call for a review of all deferments touched off a major confrontation within the Roosevelt administration as to how a decision would be made as to which workers were truly essential to the war effort. This dispute was finally resolved with an elaborate compromise that vested final authority in a committee composed of representatives of the army, navy, air force, Maritime Commission, War Production Board, War Manpower Commission, Petroleum Administration, Solid Fuels Administration, rubber director, Office of Defense Transportation, War Food Administration, and the War Shipping Administration. Each of these entities would function as a "claimant agency," submitting to the committee a list of jobs or activities within its particular sphere that were deemed essential to the war effort. The committee would then make the final decision by assigning deferment quotas to the particular agency. The numbers generated were then transmitted to local boards under a Selective Service order dated 11 April 1944, and the local boards were to accept these certifications "as strong evidence of how essential these workers were." The program proved successful in lowering the average age of recruits as those newly inducted in the below-twenty-six age group rose steadily from 44.1 percent in March to 88.1 percent in July.[8]

The pressure to limit the total numbers of occupational deferments was felt at the local level, where the Great Lakes shippers were endeavoring to find sufficient crews for the coming navigation season. At a conference held in Washington on 2 February 1944, the industry requested that the Recruitment and Manning Organization of the War Shipping Administration prepare a comprehensive plan for recruiting sailors and centralizing deferment requests for the coming season. On 24 February, the RMO submitted a proposed plan that included a recruitment program and the establishment of central lists of available personnel, from which sailors would be assigned to ships on a first-in-first-out basis. The program would also include employment stabilization features that would eliminate the movement of sailors out of the industry without special permits from the RMO; this office would also request occupational deferments for all licensed officers and able seamen regardless of age and for the possessors of other skilled ratings who were over age twenty-six. The proposed program of the RMO was immediately rejected by the bulk shippers. In a prepared statement released in response to the RMO proposal, D. C. Potts of the Pittsburgh Steamship Company noted:

> The industry has one overwhelming objection to RMO's program. The handling of deferments for Great Lakes seamen would be subordinated to an innovation for manning of Great Lakes ships. By the control of entries into the industry, the program would deprive masters of ships and management from the free selection of their personnel. This innovation would disregard traditional hiring practices in the industry and the industry would have no voice in the manning of its ships.

Potts also objected to the failure of the RMO plan to request deferments for oilers, firemen, and cooks under the age of twenty-six and to a proposal that a sailor would be considered actively employed if working seven weeks out of every eight.[9]

In order to understand the depth of industry opposition to a change in "traditional hiring practices," it is necessary to review the efforts of the maritime unions to make inroads into the Great Lakes during the war years. In 1939 and 1940, the National Maritime Union (NMU) won National Labor Relations Board (NLRB) elections in four of the smaller LCA fleets; but even after the union had been certified as the bargaining agent, it was still unsuccessful in negotiating contracts with the companies and was forced to seek assistance from the War Labor Board (WLB). The major stumbling block in the negotiations was the NMU demand for a union hiring hall, where union members would be sent to the next shipboard vacancy from a master list, and the elimination of the continuous-record discharge books ("fink books"), which, the union contended, were a built-in blacklist. While creation of a union hiring hall would have solved the impasse, President Roosevelt had declared in 1941 "that the Government of the United States will not order, nor will Congress pass, legislation ordering a so-called closed shop." Bereft of authority to order the obvious solution, the WLB issued a series of compromise orders involving maintenance of membership agreements and quotas, none of which proved effective in the peculiar circumstances of Great Lakes employment. In 1944, the WLB finally drew up a contract that included a provision to maintain union membership at the same percentage existing on 1 August 1943 and both sides were ordered to adopt it.[10]

During the 1943 season, the NMU launched a drive to unionize the largest fleet on the lakes, U.S. Steel's wholly owned subsidiary, the Pittsburgh Steamship Company. After years of frustrating negotiations with the tiny fringe companies, union leaders believed that the time was ripe to storm the LCA's strongest bastion; both sides recognized that a union victory here would spell the end of the LCA's fifty-year struggle to hold the line against organized labor on the lakes. By November, the NMU had succeeded in obtaining enough signatures to force an election, which the NLRB scheduled for June 1944. The peculiar eight-month shipping season on the Great Lakes had always posed significant problems for union organizers, whose campaigns would lag during the winter months when they had virtually no access to their potential members. By the spring of 1944, the LCA was ready with a program of propaganda and intimidation. All unlicensed personnel aboard the company's ships received two letters from Pittsburgh president A. H. Ferbert, which the NLRB later ruled were "intended and designed to discredit the Union" and "falsely posed the election issue as a contest between the Union and the respondent for the allegiance of the employees." Union organizers aboard the individual ships were threatened and ridiculed by their officers and, in at least one instance, discharged for engaging in union activities.[11]

In addition to these rather standard antiunion efforts, the company was also charged with one further stratagem that may have been decisive in the hotly contested election. During their successful unionizing efforts on the seacoasts, the NMU had staunchly opposed segregation aboard ocean vessels; but the union was understandably reticent about injecting race into their efforts on the lakes, where no African–Americans were employed other than as galley workers. During the weeks before the election, copies of an NMU pamphlet entitled *NMU Fights Jim Crow*, previously used by the union on the East Coast, were circulated among the unlicensed personnel. The union accused the company of sending out the brochures in an effort to play upon the prejudices of the white crew members. While the NLRB could find no "substantial evidence tracing responsibility for its distribution to the respondent [Pittsburgh Steamship]," it did find that one officer of the company had referred to the union as "a bunch of nigger loving bastards" and told a union organizer, "If this thing does organize and before the contract is signed I am going to hire a big nigger to be your partner and the blacker the better." Virulent racial remarks of this nature appear to have been a hallmark of the company campaign on ships throughout the fleet and were undoubtedly effective in playing upon the fears and prejudices of the sailors, who defeated the union drive by a 899 to 720 vote.[12]

Against this background, it is not difficult to understand the reluctance of the shipping industry to acquiesce in any plan that would alter their traditional hiring practices, particularly when they regarded the RMO as a bureaucratic organ under the "direct influence of the NMU." Having fought long and hard to retain control of hiring procedures, the LCA was not about to surrender that control to anyone, including a government agency. In 1945, with the WLB out of the picture, the LCA quickly broomed the NMU members from the fleet and entered the postwar era in firm control of hiring practices.[13]

Following the rejection of the RMO plan, the portion of the Great Lakes industry consisting only of the bulk cargo carriers submitted a plan of its own to be administered by the LVC. As Potts had stated, "Solution of the immediate problem lies in the effective procurement of deferment for Great Lakes seamen"; and this position was the essence of the LVC plan. All deferment requests would be made by the LVC, and deferments would be sought for:

1. licensed officers
2. seamen over twenty-two years of age certificated and employed in skilled ratings as able seamen (wheelsman, watchman, and deck watchman), oiler, and fireman
3. seamen over twenty-six years of age who are pre–Pearl Harbor fathers and employed in the ratings of cook, tunnelman, and gateman.*

Although the proposal included provisions for recruitment and stabilization, there were, of course, no mandatory hiring lists. After obtaining approval from the ODT, the LVC immediately began to administer the new program for the bulk cargo portion of the industry; however, this program did not include those companies' operating passenger ships, tankers, railroad-car ferries, package freight vessels, and the few small bulk operators not affiliated with the LCA. On 23 March 1944, no fewer than twenty-six of these entities sent a joint telegram to the ODT, requesting that that agency "establish and administer as soon as possible a coordinated plan, essentially the so-called RMO plan for the recruitment, manning and stabilization of

---

*Tunnelmen and gatemen were positions on self-unloading vessels.

employment" on the lakes. The telegram further noted that "an over-all stabilization program for all Great Lakes industry would be the answer. We offer to you our cooperation. We want a plan."[14]

On 25 March, the WSA advised the ODT that it was unwilling to undertake administration of a plan designed to aid only a portion of the Great Lakes shipping industry, noting that "such half-and-half procedure would result in so much confusion and conflict as to prohibit our acceptance of halfway responsibility." In the same letter, the WSA indicated its intention to discontinue all recruitment efforts for the industry because, in the absence of a stabilization feature, the effectiveness of such a program would "necessarily be limited." Skepticism about the effectiveness of the LVC plan also existed within the WPB, where it was felt that local draft boards would "not be much more impressed" with deferment requests from the LVC than they would be with those made by the individual companies. It was concluded, however, that "until they are sufficiently convinced of their own plight and have become dissatisfied with their own plan, . . . not a great deal can be done."[15]

The internecine strife within the industry was finally overcome at a meeting of all concerned, held in Detroit on 4 April 1944. The folly of multiple plans was recognized by all and an agreement was reached that called for the LVC to represent all Great Lakes vessel operators, including those engaged in the nonbulk trades. The stabilization program recommended by the RMO would be utilized, and that agency would also supplement recruiting efforts of the LVC. However, vessel operators would remain free to accept or reject individual sailors supplied by the RMO.[16]

As the new shipping season approached, the complex negotiations on deferment policy were the subject of numerous newspaper reports in the Great Lakes region, and dire predictions were made on the consequences of drafting lake sailors. The *Toledo Blade*, quoting an industry official, reported in March: "Unless draft boards cooperate and allow us to use crewmen in the 18 to 26 age group there will be some boats that won't leave the docks. We have only enough men to move about half of our fleet now." The *Detroit Free Press* editorialized on 15 March, "There is something wrong with our set-up when essential manufacturing, agriculture and transportation are deprived of indispensable men in order to build up fighting forces which cannot be sustained without their assistance." As late as 11 April, the Cleveland papers were reporting, "Crews of some 30 lake vessels expected to leave lower lake ports today or tomorrow are anxiously awaiting word from Washington as to their status with respect to occupational deferment." The hopes of these, and many other crews, were dashed that same day when the Selective Service System announced that deferments in the under-age-twenty-six group were limited to captains, chief engineers, and "other licensed officers for the 1944 navigation season." The decision to exclude all able seamen, as well as oilers, firemen, cooks, tunnelmen, and gatemen, had been the result of the certification process described earlier—insufficient deferments having been granted by the committee to the ODT to cover all of these groups.[17]

Despite the dire predictions, the failure of the government to provide wholesale deferments in the under-twenty-six age group did not cripple the efforts of the industry during the 1944 season. An ODT press release of 19 April reported that "95 per cent of all ships on the Lakes are moving on schedule, fully manned." A campaign of radio and newspaper advertising was utilized throughout the Midwest to recruit potential sailors, but the industry was forced to rely on "waivers" of the Coast Guard regulations to allow vessels to leave port with shortages of certificated seamen. As of 1 July, the industry reported a shortage of 197 able seamen (170 of these positions being filled by noncertificated deckhands) and 130 oilers and firemen (these positions being partially filled by 118 noncertificated coal-passers). The same report indicated that the industry fell only 81-men short of the requisite number to man all vessels fully. However, some 527 men in the eighteen-to-twenty-five age bracket were serving in nonlicensed ratings, awaiting word from their draft boards. As these men were lost to the draft, their positions were increasingly being filled by youths less than eighteen years of age who responded to the LVC advertising campaign. The LVC obtained deferments for a total of 192 licensed officers under age twenty-six, as well as 2,745 deferments for those in the twenty-six-to-thirty-seven age group.[18]

As the 1944 season drew to a close, the LVC efforts were directed toward obtaining an extension of the deferment of licensed officers in the under-twenty-six age group. While the size of this group was relatively small (193 men as of November 1944), these individuals held responsible positions and could not be easily replaced by inexperienced personnel operating under Coast Guard waivers. The LVC estimated that 3,360 licensed officers were needed to man the fleet and that the annual loss of personnel to retirement or illness was approximately two hundred, all of whom were normally replaced by able seamen in the under-twenty-six age group, who attended winter classes to obtain their licenses. This group had, of course, already been seriously whittled down by the draft, and the LVC estimated that only 40 individuals would be obtaining licenses during the coming winter months, so that normal-loss replacement would not be possible. If, in addition, all of the officers in the under-twenty-six age group were lost, "a grave emergency [would] be faced in the spring of 1945." The logic of the LVC appeal was persuasive; and in early December, General Hershey notified state directors of Selective Service that deferments for licensed officers in the under-twenty-six age group were to be continued into the 1945 navigation season.[19]

The winter of 1944–45 also featured a government program to recruit Great Lakes sailors for temporary duty on salt water to help relieve an "acute shortage of officers and seamen in off-shore shipping." As their ships were laid up for the winter months, sailors were given limited statements of availability by the USES and were urged to accept jobs on oceangoing transport. The program was voluntary, since during past winters, any sailor who preferred to remain ashore was allowed to work at a defense industry job, so that his deferment could be continued until spring. In a 1 December press release, the War Manpower Commission (WMC) announced that two hundred sailors had been recruited by the program and that at least eight hundred more were needed. By 31 January 1945, this program had become a major concern to members of the LVC, who feared that the sailors recruited off the lakes would not be returned in time to man the lake fleet in the spring, and the LVC notified the ODT that the program had to be discontinued.[20]

While the industry had survived the manpower crunch of the 1944 season with a minimum of disruption, developments on the national level would bring still more problems in 1945. The military suffered heavy casualties on the European continent during the winter campaign and the demand on the draft boards for young men continued unabated. While the program to reduce deferments in the under-twenty-six age group had been successful, the Selective Service System was reporting, in early 1945, that there simply were no potential recruits left in this age group, so the military was forced to look to the twenty-six-to-twenty-nine-year-olds to satisfy insatiable demand. As of 1 December 1944, there were some 830,000 men holding deferments in this age group; the military estimated that 255,000 of these would have to be drafted to fill quotas. Again, a major bureaucratic battle unfolded in Washington as to which agencies would control the selection process; the result was another complicated compromise. The age distinction was eliminated and everyone eighteen through twenty-nine years of age was now considered in one group. The interagency committee previously utilized was continued, but the number of deferments available to the sponsoring agencies was significantly curtailed, to 30 percent of the total number of deferments in effect as of January 1945.[21]

The impact of these decisions was made apparent on 17 February 1945, when J. M. Johnson, the new director of the ODT (the claimant agency for the Great Lakes shipping industry) circulated a letter to all employers requesting that they supply lists of all of their deferred employees under age thirty, "arranged *in order of importance*, the men whose loss would be most serious coming first on the list" (emphasis original). The 30 percent figure previously set by the interagency committee would then be applied to this list, with the balance of the men being subject to immediate induction. This procedure was to apply to all employees under age thirty, including the licensed personnel previously deferred by General Hershey's directive of the past December. Thus, the industry stood to lose some 70 percent of all licensed personnel under age thirty. On 6 March, Johnson wrote to Paul McNutt, chairman of the War Manpower Commission, advising that as a result of the new draft policy, "it is estimated by the vessel operators on the Great Lakes that sixty of their ore and grain boats cannot be placed in operation this season because of a shortage of licensed officers." Since saltwater sailors enjoyed "relative immunity" from the draft, it was likely that most of the Great Lakes sailors who had agreed to sail on the oceans during the winter months would not return to the lakes without deferment protection. Johnson proposed that the Selective Service program be altered to grant blanket deferments to all licensed personnel on the Great Lakes, while unlicensed personnel would still be subject to the 70 percent provision.[22]

On the same day as his letter to McNutt, Johnson took his campaign to the highest level, advising a meeting of the WPB that a "catastrophe . . . is impending if more manpower is taken from the transportation system" and that "60 boats, or about 20 percent of the fleet, on the Great Lakes, may be laid up for lack of skilled personnel." Johnson's efforts were rewarded in mid-March when the percentages of deferments in the transportation industries were substantially increased—to 85 percent for railroads, 80 percent for inland waterways, and 90 percent for Great Lakes carriers. The 90 percent figure was to apply to both officers and skilled seamen, with the result that the industry was able to retain virtually all licensed personnel for the coming season. In order to be eligible for such a deferment, the individual had to have been employed in his position as of the final trip of the 1944 season.[23]

The liberalized deferment policy was a significant factor in the ability of the industry successfully to man the fleet in the spring of 1945, since most of the "several thousand" Great Lakes sailors who answered the call of the offshore merchant marine returned promptly to the lakes. The combined recruiting efforts of the LVC, WMC, and USES were highly successful in attracting new employees to the industry, since "when the lakes were clear of ice, . . . not a single vessel of the fleet was held up because of lack of manpower." Once again, an influx of teenagers, too young to be subject to the draft, was important in filling the noncertificated positions. With the end of the war in Europe, pressure on the local draft boards to fill quotas began to diminish, and following V-J Day, President Truman announced that everyone over age twenty-five would be deferred from service. As a result, the industry was able to complete the 1945 season without any further manpower problems.[24]

While the companies were able to find enough men to keep the boats moving, there can be no question that overall efficiency was compromised by the influx of marginal personal. John LeCorn's 1943 difficulties aboard the *Tampico* were undoubtedly exceptional, but even the larger companies and the bigger ships had problems aplenty. A mate in the Columbia fleet remembers working six hours on and six hours off because a third mate could not be found, while Perry Klumph recalled leading a watch aboard a Pittsburgh boat in 1945: "My wheelsman was a first year AB, never been in a pilot house, my watchman was a short-order cook out of a restaurant, my deckwatch was out of the hills of Tennessee, the three deckhands were Florida crackers (teenagers). They had tennis shoes on. They had never seen so much money as they were going to make until we got up to the cold weather, then they left in a hurry." Similar problems existed on the after end. Hubert Kessel would sometimes have to "just tell [the oilers] to sit down and you would oil the engine yourself because you didn't want them to fall in."[25]

John LeCorn's drunken engineer was certainly not an isolated case, for drinking and discipline problems beset the fleet. While a ship was loading ore at the head the lakes, the third mate and the third assistant engineer often drew the unsavory task of rounding up inebriated crew members from the waterfront bars of Duluth or Superior. Shipboard maintenance usually suffered, since crew members refused to do much of the normal scraping, painting, and scrubbing. It is little wonder that one veteran mate remembered the wartime replacements as predominately "drunks and snotty kids."[26]

In many ways, the manpower shortages that beset the Great Lakes shipping industry were typical of those seen throughout the American economy during the war years. The nation struggled to shift gears from bread lines to maximum employment, to put in place a bureaucratic structure for evaluating and prioritizing competing manpower demands. Like most other employers, Great Lakes shippers considered their employment needs critical and essential to the war effort, and they made repeated demands on the government for special considerations. For the most part, however, they were able to man their vessels successfully with a minimum of governmental involvement. Unlike their oceangoing counterparts, they did not enjoy the benefits of blanket deferments; those deferments that were granted to licensed personnel encompassed a relatively small number of individuals who held special skills, truly essential to the war effort. Government programs were employed for recruitment and stabilization, but these endeavors were widely used in various segments of the wartime economy. The 1944 rejection of the RMO plan was, of course, motivated by the industry's selfish desire to maintain traditional hiring practices; yet regardless of motivation, the industry did devise and successfully implement its own plan to meet the manpower crisis.

While the shortage of personnel certainly compromised maintenance and efficiency, there was not a single instance of a ship's failing to sail for lack of crew. Much of the credit for the success of the Great Lakes shippers in meeting their wartime goals must be given to the relative handful of veteran lake officers and sailors who were able to keep their boats running despite the manpower crisis.

6
Wartime Construction

Endless money forms the sinews of war.
—Cicero, 44 B.C.

Cost is not controlling in this emergency.
—Ralph Budd, 1940

nder the perceived pressures of wartime expedience, the federal government roared out of the Depression mindset with a barrage of spending
never before seen in the nation's history. A fivefold increase funded programs large and small, both directly and indirectly related to military expansion; but the common thread throughout was necessity dictated by national
security. In this atmosphere, waste was inevitable; and an obscure, former
haberdasher from Missouri named Harry S. Truman rose to national promi-
nence chairing the Senate Special Committee to Investigate the National Defense Program. Truman's committee probed for "incompetence, waste or
mismanagement"—and there was plenty of each to go around.[1]

All over the country, legislators pushed pork-barrel priorities, hoping to
have their particular area share in the extraordinary flow of money from
Washington. The proposed programs ranged from the ridiculous to the sub-
lime (some were both), and the Great Lakes region had its share of each.
While the Sault Ste. Marie Chamber of Commerce pushed airport expansion
as a key to adequate protection for the locks, Green Bay businessmen were
convinced that their port was "unquestionably preferable" to any other for
development as a major iron-ore shipping center. Perhaps the boldest
suggestion of all came from William E. Scripps, president of the *Detroit
News*, who urged the "developing on the south shore of the Upper Peninsula
of plants that would make possible the smelting of ore direct from the

mines." While such a move was offered as a way to avoid the transportation danger of the Soo Locks bottleneck, it would also happen to have the additional effect of transferring to Michigan a considerable portion of the nation's steel industry. While these proposals were never acted upon, several capital-improvement projects of major significance to the Great Lakes shipping industry were funded during the war years. How some of these developments came about demonstrates, again, the close, working relationship that existed between government and industry on the lakes.[2]

The MacArthur Lock

One of the most important of these projects—and one heartily endorsed by the Lake Carriers Association—was the construction of the MacArthur Lock at the Soo. On the eve of war, the lock system in existence at the Soo functioned with reasonable efficiency in raising and lowering commercial traffic between the levels of Lakes Superior and Huron. The St. Marys River, which connected these lakes, ran in an east–west direction at the rapids, separating the twin cities of Sault Ste. Marie, Ontario to the north and Sault Ste. Marie, Michigan to the south. The vast majority of commercial traffic funneled through the four locks on the American side of the channel. The two northernmost locks, the Davis and the Sabin, were 1,350 feet long, 80 feet wide, and 24.5 feet deep; the Poe Lock, completed in 1896, was 800 feet long, 100 feet wide, but only 17 feet deep. The last lock, the Weitzel, was considered obsolete and was no longer utilized because of its 11 foot depth. One additional lock existed, on the Canadian side of the river; but this channel was also very shallow and was little utilized for commercial traffic. Loaded vessels normally locked down through the Davis or Sabin Locks; vessels returning to Lake Superior without cargo would be sent through the Poe; and recreational traffic and smaller commercial vessels would lock through on the Canadian side.[3]

This system functioned reasonably well. Even though the facilities were many years old, they were in good repair, and there was no indication that use of the locks was nearing a saturation point. The motive for the construction of a new lock was an interesting combination of the dictates of public necessity and the quest for increased private profit. The railroad accident of 7 October 1941 had underscored the peculiar susceptibility of the industry to any disruption of this commercial artery, and the addition of another deep lock was seen as a prudent safeguard. However, the LCA also recognized that a new lock, constructed to a greater depth than that of the Sabin or Davis Lock, would allow ships of greater draft to transit the system and yield significantly more economical operation. Given the impetus of national security, the industry was able to weave these two strands into a new lock with considerable dispatch.

In a letter to Ralph Budd dated 30 December 1940, A. T. Wood first broached the topic, suggesting that "the construction of a new lock . . . would form an important addition to the lockage facilities whenever the traffic is such as to tax the present lockage system." Wood went on to suggest that the first step toward completion of such was to refer the matter to the River and Harbor Committee of the House of Representatives for further study. That committee quickly assigned the matter to the U.S. Army Corps of Engineers, who promptly contacted the LCA, "requesting [their] views in the premises." On 24 February 1941, LCA vice-president L. C. Sabin responded with a detailed, five-page report, setting forth the LCA's suggestions for the new lock. After citing statistics on vessel use, Sabin acknowledged that there was "only slight evidence that the reasonable capacity of the three locks in service [was] being reached" and that the figures did "not indicate a close approach to reasonable capacity." Yet these same statistics amply demonstrated that "the crippling of one lock would have serious results . . . at the traffic level now prevailing." After placing the case for a new lock on a solid, national security footing, Sabin went on to state the other LCA concern: "The construction of a new lock at St. Marys Falls Canal being required primarily to serve as insurance against serious interruption of traffic should also fill the coming need of increased depth. Its construction would be the most expensive item in making provision for the utilization of deeper draft ships now beginning to receive consideration." Sabin went on to suggest that the new lock be constructed on the site of the obsolete Weitzel Lock and that its dimensions be 860 feet long, 80 feet wide, and 30 feet deep.[4]

Funding for the proposed lock was originally included in the 1941 omnibus rivers-and-harbors bill, which included "a large number of items, some of which are of doubtful merit," and Wood sought to have the measure removed from this morass and introduced separately. The accident at the Soo added weight to Wood's arguments, and his direct appeal to Michigan Senator Prentiss Brown proved successful when Brown added the lock funding as an amendment to a naval pay bill, which received legislative approval in February of 1942. The lock, as approved, was virtually identical to that proposed by Sabin one year earlier. Construction was begun immediately, with the cost set at eight million dollars. Under the pressure of wartime demands, work proceeded at a frantic pace, with more than one thousand workers employed on the project. In order to work through the winter months, engineers designed plywood structures to be built over each section of the lock; and electric blowers were utilized to heat these buildings, thus allowing the workers to continue to pour cement despite the extreme cold of the Sault Ste. Marie winter. Construction was completed—and the lock filled with water— on 2 July 1943, two days ahead of schedule. A dedication ceremony was held on 11 July, the new facility being named after General Douglas MacArthur.[5]

The successful construction of the MacArthur Lock was the result of a near-perfect blend of government and industry interests. The lock functioned efficiently during the balance of the war years, while providing the nation with additional insurance against disruption to the flow of iron ore. From the industry standpoint, subsequent vessel construction would incorporate the deeper draft made possible by the construction of the MacArthur Lock, thus allowing a significant increase in capacity per trip with a minimum of increased cost.*

The Escanaba Bypass

Unfortunately, there were other construction projects undertaken during the war years that did not exhibit the level of industry–government cooperation shown in the construction of the MacArthur Lock. The effort to develop the port of Escanaba as additional insurance against major disruption at the Soo was an undertaking fraught with misunderstanding and controversy from beginning to end. This port, located at the north end of Lake Michigan, on the southern shore of Michigan's Upper Peninsula, was the only iron ore shipping facility located below the Soo Locks. The city was close enough to the Michigan iron-ore ranges to allow for the economical shipment of small amounts of ore, but the bulk of the ore deposits located in the larger Minnesota ranges could be more economically shipped from the ports located on Lake Superior. During the war's early months, the military, in cooperation with the Great Lakes shipping industry, had gone to great lengths to safeguard the locks at Sault Ste. Marie, while the construction of the MacArthur Lock provided additional insurance against sabotage or accident. The fact remained, however, that the supply of iron ore could be shut off by a successful attack at the Soo; and this point fueled interest in the development of some form of alternative measure that would not be so susceptible to enemy action.

---

*The MacArthur Lock is still functioning as an important component of the lock system. In 1969, the Poe Lock was reconstructed to allow for the passage of lake freighters 105 feet wide and in excess of 1,000 feet long. Fourteen of these vessels are in operation today. With this exception, the lock system still functions as described in this chapter.

This problem drew the attention of President Roosevelt himself: in December 1940, he ordered an engineering study of a proposal to construct an "overland ship railway" around the locks. Under this plan, fully loaded ore carriers would be hoisted out of the water on the Lake Superior side and placed aboard specially designed trains for transit around the falls of the St. Marys River. (While the documents indicate only that they were prepared "at the personal request of the President," it is difficult to resist the image of the self-confident, still robust chief executive, cigarette holder clamped at a jaunty angle, barking: "Why don't we just pick those damn boats up and carry them around the rapids? Get me a report on that!") The results of the engineering study were predictably disappointing. Great Lakes freighters were too "frail" to stand the structural stresses of being lifted out of the water fully loaded; and even if the concept were technically feasible, the engineers found it "difficult to conceive of a successful operation of the magnitude that would be required to handle 15,000 boats in 210 days." As an alternative to the "ship railway," the engineers went on to tout development of the port of Escanaba.[6]

Another bypass method given some consideration was the construction of a conveyor system around the locks, but this proposal also had numerous flaws. Engineers estimated that such a system would take a minimum of eighteen months to construct at a cost of some one hundred thousand dollars and use enormous amounts of precious steel and rubber, while its location alongside the existing locks would make it equally vulnerable to destruction by enemy action.[7]

It soon appeared to transportation officials that if any alternative to the locks was to be created, Escanaba would be central to the plan. On 9 March 1942, Senator Brown, trumpeting the Escanaba alternative, told the *Detroit News*, "There can be no real danger to transportation from the north shores of Lake Michigan and Huron [sic] because there are no canals, locks, etc., between these points and the production areas in Detroit, Chicago, and the Ohio–Pennsylvania areas." On 1 June 1942, Michigan's governor, Murray D. Van Wagoner, urged the further development of the Escanaba facilities in a telegram to ODT director Eastman, pointing out that the expenditure of four to five million dollars would double the capacity of the port.[8]

The possibility of constructing an alternative route for the iron ore shipments was considered by the WPB at its meeting of 4 August 1942, when a group with the rather ponderous title of the Committee to Consider the Need for a Transportation Alternative to the Soo Locks for the Movement of Iron Ore issued its report. The committee reviewed the now-familiar facts on the importance of the Soo bottleneck and the measures in place to guard against direct attack or sabotage and warned that a successful enemy action could close the canal for an entire shipping season. Such an eventuality would result in the necessity of moving the iron ore by rail, a process that would be "extraordinarily expensive" and that would "gravely affect the coal movement and the flow of many other vital war materials." As "partial insurance against [such a] contingency," the committee recommended

1. the immediate construction of ore docks and yards and the possible dredging of necessary channels at Escanaba, Michigan, for the handling of sixty million tons of iron ore per season
2. the immediate improvement through the ballasting, tying, and strengthening of bridges of the railroad beds operating between Superior and Escanaba and between Ironwood, Michigan, and Escanaba.

The committee had been assured by the ODT that the remaining thirty to forty million tons of ore required annually by the steel industry could be moved by rail. The cost of the project was pegged at $22,411,000, plus dredging as necessary. The improvements were to be completed by April 1943, thus helping to "ease the strain" on the other shipping ports anticipated for the 1943 season. The committee also recommended, however, that some of the heavier steel rails not be installed unless and until an emergency actually developed; and the subsequent ratification of the proposal contained a limitation of five thousand tons of critical steel for the entire project.[9]

Following approval by the War Production Board, the plan was immediately enveloped in the extraordinary haze of the Washington wartime bureaucracy. On 31 August, Secretary of Commerce Jesse Jones informed WPB chairman Donald Nelson that army engineers did not concur in the estimates provided by the committee and that in fact, the project would consume "far in excess" of the five thousand tons of critical materials estimated and that the cost would run to some forty-eight million dollars. After additional meetings, the committee revised its plan into two "phases." Phase 1 would encompass all work necessary to bring the project within sixty days of completion, including the construction of two new loading docks, the driving of piling to support two additional docks, the construction of staging yards adjacent to the docks, and the ballasting and tying of roadbeds and strengthening of bridges on the railroad lines between Superior, Wisconsin, and Escanaba. Phase 2 essentially encompassed the planning necessary to complete the project should the emergency arise and included provisions for borrowing unloading equipment from Lake Superior loading docks and for actually installing new rail along the route from Wisconsin. It is important to note that even at this early stage, the entire project was viewed by those involved as no more than an emergency backup to the locks at Sault Ste. Marie and there was no plan to utilize the new docks unless and until an emergency actually occurred.[10]

Following WPB approval of the revised plan, the same was submitted to the Facilities Clearance Board, an administrative arm of the WPB whose function was to assign priority ratings to new construction. On 14 October, this board unanimously chose to second-guess the WPB when it found that the Escanaba project was "too expensive in terms of critical materials to be justified (even if only Phase #1 were approved)," because "a policy of providing standby facilities cannot be implemented with critical materials at this time without hindering the war production effort." This decision was subsequently appealed and reversed; but the AA-4 priority rating granted to the project on 23 October was a severe disappointment to A. F. Shafter, the chairman of the Escanaba Committee, who subsequently resigned in protest. By the time the haggling over priorities was resolved, the project was far behind schedule—and it was apparent that not even Phase 1 would be ready by the following spring.[11]

The WPB announcement of the plan to erect new loading facilities had been greeted with enthusiasm in Escanaba, and throughout Michigan's Upper Peninsula, since the area hoped to enjoy not only the temporary benefits of the building boom but a larger, more significant role in the postwar iron ore industry. Although the project had never been intended as anything more than insurance against loss of the Soo Locks, this fact was not publicized, because the WPB did not wish to draw attention to the vulnerability of the locks, leading a WPB official later to lament, "It was, therefore, impossible to counteract earlier the false impression that this project was intended as a normal operating device." Construction on the project began in October 1942; soon after over twenty-five hundred workers were employed, transforming Escanaba into one of the war's boom towns. A giant, wooden loading dock, 1,800 feet long, 60 feet wide, and 80 feet high, was constructed in a few months time, while work progressed on the foundation for a second, similar structure and on the railroad improvements necessary to transport the ore to the docks.[12]

But the boom-town atmosphere in Escanaba was to be short-lived. During the winter of 1942/43, serious, unanticipated shortages of the lumber used for railroad ties and structural timber occurred as a result of severe weather and labor shortages in the Pacific Northwest, causing all railroad maintenance materials to be upgraded to an AA-1 rating. In addition, some of the basic assumptions underlying the Escanaba expenditures were being reexamined in Washington. With the military's downgrading its assessment of the threat to the Sault Ste. Marie area and the MacArthur lock nearing completion, the danger of interruption at the Soo was seen as much less significant than it had been during the traumatic opening months of the war. Also, while some work had been completed on the necessary railroad beds and bridges, the shortage of heavy rails had prevented the completion of the 360 miles of rail necessary to link the city with the iron ore ranges. In April, WPB chairman Donald Nelson ordered work on the second dock discontinued, while the first structure (which was essentially finished except for the installation of steel chutes) was to be left within sixty days of completion. The two partially completed docks were never utilized, and the government ordered the second dock dismantled in November of 1944, the huge wooden beams being sawed into lumber for use in constructing barracks and an ordinance plant. The remaining dock was razed in the summer of 1945 and the entire 1,986-acre tract was sold by the federal government to the City of Escanaba in 1946 for sixty-five thousand dollars.[13]

The decision to abandon the project was a stunning blow to the local economy, and there were those who saw preservation of postwar competitive advantage as the motive. In a widely circulated article originally published in the *Baltimore Sun*, columnist A. A. Imberman accused the U.S. Steel Corporation of blocking completion of the Escanaba project so that it could maintain a competitive advantage by continuing to ship ore from the mines to the docks in Superior–Duluth on its wholly owned Duluth, Missabe, and Northern Railroad, "not so much now as in the postwar years when competition on prices is important." It would seem more likely, however, that the Escanaba alternative was doomed from the beginning, by both the shortage of critical steel and by the economics of iron ore transportation. The greater distance involved for railroad shipment from most parts of the iron ore ranges to Escanaba would have had the overall effect of adding to the cost of transporting each ton of ore, since water transportation of bulk commodities is significantly cheaper than by rail. The LCA estimated in 1940 that the rate for moving ore from the Minnesota ranges to the lower lake ports and the Chicago area was $1.76 per ton via the Soo, as compared to $3.71 per ton by rail. This fact had caused the LCA to conclude, as early as 21 December 1940, that "the proposed additional ore dock at Escanaba and all rail ore movement to that port from Minnesota mines for lake shipment [is] considered to be unsound." The decision of the WPB to develop the Escanaba alternative was simply an insurance measure against disaster at the Soo. It never had enthusiastic support from Great Lakes shippers nor any possibility of providing the Escanaba region with a competitive advantage in the postwar economy.[14]

U.S. Coast Guard Icebreaker *Mackinaw*

Another federally funded, wartime construction project that drew a less-than-enthusiastic response from the Great Lakes shipping industry was the building of the Coast Guard cutter *Mackinaw*. The decision to build a state-of-the-art icebreaker for the Great Lakes, with a price tag estimated at eight million dollars, was announced by the government on 20 February 1942. When the ship was launched in the fall of 1944, the total cost had risen to a whopping ten million dollars, over five times the cost of a standard freighter and two million dollars more than the cost of the MacArthur Lock. The ship was 290 feet long with a 75 foot beam—dimensions that effectively land-locked the ship to the Great Lakes—and was powered by diesel engines to-taling ten thousand horsepower. Many ice-breaking innovations were included in the vessel's design, including a bow-mounted propeller that churned the water under the ice (to change its static buoyancy and make it easier to crush) and a heeling system that pumped water from one side of the ship to the other at the rate of one ton per second, thus allowing a rocking motion that would free the ship from ice. The *Mackinaw* would carry a crew of 12 officers and 164 other men.[15]

The construction of the *Mackinaw* was a war measure, and the stated justification for its incredible cost was the need to extend the shipping season to the greatest length possible in order to meet the established iron ore quotas. The assumption was that the new icebreaker would be able effectively to clear a channel through the heavy, windrowed ice of Whitefish Bay and the St. Marys River in late March or early April, so that the industry would no longer be forced to wait for mild weather before beginning the season. There were those in the shipping industry, however, who doubted the wisdom of spending such a large sum on one vessel, pointing out that winter's grip ex-tended over many places on the Great Lakes simultaneously and that "the centralization of facility in one ship [was] ill-judged and the enormous cost [was] extravagance."[16]

Commissioned in the fall of 1944, the ship was available for duty at the end of the 1944 season. However, unusually mild temperatures allowed ves-sel operations to extend into December without the need for icebreaking. During the month of January 1945, the *Mackinaw* escorted three oceangoing cargo vessels, recently completed at Duluth–Superior, to Chicago, for ulti-mate delivery to New Orleans through the Illinois–Mississippi Waterway. Later that same month, the cutter escorted the brand-new auxiliary de-stroyer *Donald W. Wolf* from the shipyard at Bay City, Michigan, to Chicago for a similar trip down the Mississippi to New Orleans. During this time pe-riod, the ship also served as a special training vessel, hosting officers of the

99

Russian Navy, who were observing operational procedure in preparation for the delivery of four modern U.S. Coast Guard icebreakers to our Soviet allies under the lend-lease program. The *Mackinaw* took part in icebreaking at the beginning of the 1945 season, but the unusually mild conditions again rendered these operations secondary to the natural disintegration. Thus, the overall contribution of the *Mackinaw* to the war effort was negligible.[17]*

Government Fleet Expansion Incentives and the Maritime Class

One further capital improvement to the shipping industry that came about during the war years was the addition to the iron ore fleet of twenty-one new bulk freighters, the construction of which was due in large measure to government initiative and subsidy. During the Depression years, shipbuilding on the Great Lakes came to a virtual halt, since companies were far more concerned with finding cargos for their existing bottoms than with constructing new ones. Four bulk carriers delivered to the Pittsburgh Steamship Company in 1938 were the only new vessels commissioned in the ore trade from 1930 through 1941. The lack of a shipbuilding program was an even greater concern with the nation's oceangoing fleet, which had been allowed to decay since the end of World War I, a condition that Congress sought to alleviate with the passage of the Merchant Marine Act of 1936. This act created the U.S. Maritime Commission and provided for a ship construction fund "to stabilize shipbuilding and ship operating and to encourage the building of a modern merchant fleet able to compete with the ships of other nations, and to provide a source for military and naval auxiliaries in time of war." Title V of the act provided for a "construction differential subsidy," under which the government would pay for a new vessel to the extent that the cost of the domestically built ship exceeded the cost in a foreign shipyard and would finance the remaining cost for the owner at very reasonable rates. By 1937, a program to build fifty new oceangoing vessels per year was under way.[18]

Although the Merchant Marine Act of 1936 was critical to the rebirth of the nation's ocean fleet, by its terms, the 1936 act had no application to domestic commerce. In 1939, the act was amended to include Section 510,

---

*The *Mackinaw* remains the largest U.S.-flag icebreaker on the Great Lakes. An important contributor to the economy of its home port of Cheboygan, the ship is the subject matter of frequent budget battles, with criticism centering on the ship's large operating cost.

which authorized the Maritime Commission to "acquire any obsolete vessel in exchange for an allowance of credit"—which could be used by the owner as a down payment on new construction. This new section was made applicable to "the domestic and foreign water-borne commerce of the United States." The act was amended again in October of 1940 to authorize "construction reserve funds," which allowed shipping companies to shield funds from federal excess profit taxes, provided that the money was used in the construction of a new ship within two years.[19]

These measures provided significant incentives to Great Lakes companies interested in fleet expansion, and the giant Pittsburgh Steamship Company became the first to take advantage when it announced plans for five new carriers in March of 1941. Three of the ships were to be built at Great Lakes Engineering Works in River Rouge, Michigan; two, at the American Shipbuilding Company of Lorain, Ohio. When delivered in 1942, they would be the largest ships ever to operate on the lakes, at 640 feet long and 67 feet wide; and their cargo capacity, at a maximum draft of 23 feet, would approach 17,500 gross tons. Pursuant to the amended Merchant Marine Act, the company utilized a construction reserve fund for payment, thus enjoying what amounted to a federal subsidy through the tax savings. These five ships (collectively known as the Fraser Class) joined the fleet during the 1942 season, in time to make a significant contribution toward the tonnage record achieved that year:[20]

1. *Leon Fraser.* Converted to oil by American Shipbuilding Co., 1970. Shortened 120 feet and converted to a self-unloading cement carrier at Fraser Shipyards, Superior, Wisconsin, 1991. Now owned by Inland Lakes Transportation.
2. *Enders M. Voorhees.* Converted to oil by Bay Shipbuilding Co., 1973. Sold for scrap, 1987.
3. *A. H. Ferbert.* Converted to oil by DeFoe Shipbuilding Co., 1972. Sold for scrap, 1987.
4. *Benjamin F. Fairless.* Converted to oil by DeFoe Shipbuilding Co., 1973. Sold for scrap, 1988.
5. *Irving S. Olds.* Converted to oil by Fraser Shipyards, 1974. Sold for scrap, 1988.

During 1941, the American steel industry finally came to grips with the need for a rapid and significant increase in the nation's steel production capacity, a necessary corollary of which was the expansion of the Great Lakes fleet needed to provide the raw materials for that increase. The Office of Production Management released an analysis in August, predicting that at least twenty-five new freighters would be needed to provide sufficient vessel capacity for the steel expansion program and pegging the construction cost of the ships at fifty million dollars. However, a committee of the LCA, which had been assigned the task of examining the proposal from the industry standpoint, took exception with the conclusions of the OPM report, contending that fewer vessels would be needed. There was also significant debate over whether the new ships would be built with government funds or paid for by the ultimate owners. Even within the industry itself, no consensus could be reached on a standard design for the proposed freighters.[21]

On 5 September, Maritime Commission chairman Emory S. Land provided LCA president Wood with the terms of a program for commission subsidization of the construction of the new ore carriers. Under this proposal, Great Lakes vessel operators would trade in "obsolete vessels" to the commission and would receive a credit toward the purchase of the new vessel of $63.75 per gross ton of ore-carrying capacity up to a maximum of 110 percent of the capacity of the new ship. The obsolete vessels would then be leased back to the operators under a typical bare-boat charter agreement at a cost of $2.50 per ton of carrying capacity. The individual companies were to contract directly with the shipyards for the construction of the new ships and were free to specify their own designs, while the commission would finance the purchase at attractive interest rates.[22]

While these terms were appealing to the vessel operators, they immediately ran into difficulties with the shipbuilders, who, because of the extraordinary increases in material and labor costs they were experiencing, refused to bid the contracts on a fixed-price basis, demanding, instead, an escalator clause that would pass any cost increases incurred during construction on to the owners. The LCA went back to the Maritime Commission and attempted to negotiate an additional term to their agreement that would have had the Commission bearing the burden of any increase in cost during construction beyond a fixed price; but this offer was rejected by the commission with the comment, "It was necessary for your companies, as any other business man under present conditions, to assume some risks in connection with the enterprise." In the opinion of the commissioners, the trade-in allowances provided were liberal, and they would not "underwrite a ceiling on the adjusted cost of the vessels."[23]

On 9 October 1941, Maritime Commission assistant director Howard L. Vickery presented a memorandum to the commission stating:

> Although the construction of ore vessels has been under discussion with representatives of the Lake Carriers Association for several months, the members of the Association have failed to present an acceptable proposal,

notwithstanding that it has been determined that the immediate construction of sixteen ore carriers as an addition to the existing Great Lakes ore fleet is essential to the success of the National Defense Program. In fact, yesterday the President of the Association advised me that the operators have abandoned their efforts to formulate a construction program.

Vickery went on to recommend that the Maritime Commission negotiate directly with the shipyards for the construction of the sixteen ore carriers 604 feet long and 60 feet wide, at a cost not to exceed $1,986,000 per vessel. Without the need for industry consensus, Vickery moved with dispatch. At a special meeting on 11 October, the commission awarded a contract to the American Shipbuilding Company for the construction of four bulk freighters at its Lorain facility and two more at its Cleveland yard at a unit price of $1,972,000 all six vessels to be delivered between 1 April and 15 June 1943. On 14 October, the commission awarded a similar contract to the Great Lakes Engineering Works for an additional ten ships, six to be completed at River Rouge, Michigan, four, at Ashtabula, Ohio, all vessels to be delivered by 1 July 1943. Of great significance to the shipping companies, the sixteen ships were to be equipped with reciprocating engines, rather than state-of-the-art turbine propulsion, because of a shortage in turbine machinery. This fact would render the Maritime Class vessels slower and less fuel-efficient than the recently completed Fraser Class.[24]

Having presented the shipping companies with a fait accompli, Vickery felt confident that the Great Lakes vessel operators would purchase the new ships, rather than run the competitive risk of having sixteen new vessels owned by the government "loose on the lakes"; but the great cost of the vessels and the presence of the reciprocating engines left the companies wary. Finally, in June of 1942, the companies again approached the commission, and negotiations resumed with the commission's original proposal of 5 September 1941 remaining as the basis for discussion. Nine vessel operators eventually agreed to purchase the sixteen freighters under Section 509 of the Merchant Marine Act, and the commission agreed to accept thirty-six ships as trade-ins (see Table 1) under Section 510 and to lease them back to the companies until the end of the war, when the law required that they be scrapped. In addition, the parties agreed that should a completed ship have a total price tag in excess of $2,250,000, either party would be free to cancel the sale. By purchasing the new vessels, the companies had protected themselves against the threat of a significant increase in fleet capacity in the postwar era, a condition that could have been ruinous from a competitive standpoint, while the Maritime Commission succeeded in its goal of bringing about an immediate increase in fleet capacity.[25]

Table 1. Vessels Traded to United States Maritime Commission

Ship	Owner	Year Built	Capacity (Tons)
A. W. Osborne	Wilson Transit	1897	6,200
Kickapoo	Wilson Transit	1900	5,560
Superior	Reiss Steamship	1901	7,000
Alex B. Uhrig	Reiss Steamship	1893	4,900
Herman C. Strom	Pittsburgh Steamship	1903	7,200
Queen City	Pittsburgh Steamship	1896	6,400
Pentecost Mitchell	Pittsburgh Steamship	1903	6,800
Robert Fulton	Pittsburgh Steamship	1896	6,000
Clarence A. Black	Pittsburgh Steamship	1898	7,200
Rensselaer	Pittsburgh Steamship	1900	7,800
Zenith City	Pittsburgh Steamship	1895	6,000
Corvus	Interlake Steamship	1903	6,900
Cygnus	Interlake Steamship	1903	6,900
Pegasus	Interlake Steamship	1902	6,800
Saturn	Interlake Steamship	1901	6,800
Taurus	Interlake Steamship	1903	6,900
Vega	Interlake Steamship	1906	7,000
Cetus	Interlake Steamship	1903	6,900
Chacornac	Cleveland–Cliffs	1902	6,200
Colonel	Fontana S. S. (Cliffs)	1901	5,800
Yosemite	Fontana S. S. (Cliffs)	1901	5,800
Munising	Cleveland–Cliffs	1902	6,400
Negaunee	Cleveland–Cliffs	1902	6,200
Maritana	Buckeye Steamship	1892	4,300
Mariposa	Buckeye Steamship	1892	4,300
Alexander McDougall	Buckeye Steamship	1898	6,900
B. Lyman Smith	Great Lakes Steamship	1903	6,300
George B. Leonard	Great Lakes Steamship	1903	6,300
William Nottingham	Great Lakes Steamship	1902	6,300
Wilbert L. Smith	Great Lakes Steamship	1903	6,300
Monroe C. Smith	Great Lakes Steamship	1903	6,300
Amazon	Hutchinson and Company	1897	5,700
S.B. Coolidge	Pioneer Steamship	1897	5,700
Saucon	Bethlehem Transportation	1906	11,000
Cornwall	Bethlehem Transportation	1907	9,800
Johnstown	Bethlehem Transportation	1905	10,600

In attempting to evaluate these purchases from the standpoint of the shipping companies the experience of the Wilson Transit Company is instructive. The company purchased one ship from the Maritime Commission, the *Thomas Wilson*, at a total purchase price of $2,214,725 and received a credit of $888,803 by trading in the steamers *Captain Thomas Wilson* (renamed *Kickapoo* after the trade) and *A. W. Osborne*, thus making a net payment of $1,325,922 for the new ship, an amount financed by the commission at 3.5 percent interest. This amount compares quite favorably with the $2,112,248 cost of the Fraser Class ships even when the lack of turbine propulsion is considered. Additionally, the company continued to operate the two "obsolete vessels" until the ore demand began to slacken, showing a net profit from the two ships of $128,397 for the balance of the 1943 season.[26]

The sixteen ships of the Maritime Class were all delivered to their new owners during the difficult 1943 season, although the last two did not depart on their maiden voyages until November. The Pittsburgh Steamship Company and the Interlake Steamship Company purchased three ships each, with seven other companies absorbing the remaining ten boats:

1. *J. Burton Ayers*. Originally purchased by Great Lakes Steamship Co. Currently operated by Columbia Transportation. Converted to self-unloader, 1974. Converted to oil, 1975.
2. *George A. Sloan*. Originally purchased by Pittsburgh Steamship Co., currently operated by their successor, U.S. Steel. Converted to self-unloader, 1967. Converted to oil, 1977. Repowered, 1985.
3. *Richard J. Reiss*. Originally purchased by Reiss Steamship Co. Currently operated by Erie Sand Steamship Co. Converted to self-unloader, 1964. Converted to diesel, 1976.
4. *Crispin Oglebay* (*J. H. Hillman, Jr.*, 1943–74). Originally purchased by Great Lakes Steamship Co. Currently operated by Columbia Transportation. Converted to self-unloader, 1978.
5. *Robert C. Norton* (*Steelton*, 1943–66; *Frank Purnell*, 1966–74). Originally purchased by Bethlehem Transportation Co. Currently owned by Columbia Transportation. Converted to self-unloader, 1966.
6. *Willowglen* (*Lehigh*, 1943–81; *Joseph X. Robert*, 1981–82). Originally purchased by Bethlehem Transportation Co. Currently operated by P&H Shipping.
7. *Pioneer* (*Frank Purnell*, 1943–66; *Steelton*, 1966–78). Originally purchased by Interlake Steamship Co. Converted to oil, 1971. Permanently laid up for use as storage facility, 1982.
8. *E. G. Grace*. Originally purchased by Interlake Steamship Co. Sold for scrap, 1984.

9. *John T. Hutchinson.* Originally purchased by Buckeye Steamship Co. Converted to self-unloader, 1964. Sold for scrap, 1988.
10. *Robert C. Stanley.* Originally purchased by Pittsburgh Steamship Co. Converted to oil, 1975. Sold for scrap, 1987.
11. *Samuel Mather* (*Frank Armstrong,* 1943–76). Originally purchased by Interlake Steamship Co. Converted to oil, 1973. Sold for scrap, 1988.
12. *Ashland* (*Clarence B. Randall,* 1943–62). Originally purchased by Pioneer Steamship Co. Sold for scrap, 1988.
13. *Thomas Wilson.* Originally purchased by Wilson Transit Co. Converted to oil, 1977. Sold for scrap, 1988.
14. *Sewell Avery.* Originally purchased by Pittsburgh Steamship Co. Converted to oil, 1973. Sold for scrap, 1986.
15. *Champlain.* Originally purchased by Cleveland–Cliffs Iron Co. Sold for scrap, 1986.
16. *Cadillac.* Originally purchased by Cleveland–Cliffs Iron Co. Sold for scrap, 1986.

The contribution of these ships helped to limit the impact of the bad fortune that plagued the industry that year.*

The twenty-one bulk freighters added to the Great Lakes fleet during the war years represented a significant modernization of the industry, and there can be no question that through the tax benefits and the Section 510 trade-in provisions the government significantly subsidized that modernization. Yet the amount of public funds expended pales in comparison to that lavished on other critical industries. For example, Francis Walton estimates that 60 percent of the seven hundred million dollars spent for steel industry expansion in 1943 was direct government investment. Overall, the capital improvements to the Great Lakes shipping industry spurred by wartime necessity, while important to the individual operators, were an insignificant trickle in the torrent of federal spending.[27]

---

*As of the start of the 1992 shipping season, six of the sixteen Maritime Class vessels were still registered on the Great Lakes, five of them having been converted to self-unloaders. Four of the five vessels of the Fraser Class have been scrapped, and the remaining one (the *Leon Fraser*) was recently converted to a cement carrier.

Conclusion

... World War Two, an event that changed the psyche as well as the
face of the United States and the World.

—Studs Terkel

World War II was a catalyst for economic and cultural change on a massive
scale throughout the United States. The nation was able to leave behind the
gnawing doubt fostered by the Great Depression and reaffirm the strength
and integrity of democratic capitalism, with pent-up consumer demand fuel-
ing rapid economic expansion. The federal government emerged from the
war with an enormously expanded role in the daily lives of its citizens, while
big business and the military began a cooperative arrangement that would
come to dominate the Cold War era. Personal income rose from $72.6 bil-
lion in 1939 to $172 billion in 1945, bringing about a significant redistribu-
tion of wealth that converted the United States to a middle-class country.
Organized labor gained acceptance as a major player in American society,
memberships increasing from nine million in 1941, to fifteen million by
1945, while the demand for production workers caused a migration to the
metropolitan areas and provided blacks and women with unprecedented
employment opportunities.[1]

The crucible of war brought change to all segments of the economy, and
the Great Lakes shipping industry was no exception. The completion of the
MacArthur Lock allowed vessel owners significantly to increase the trip capacity of their ships, and the next generation of lake freighters to be constructed would be designed to take advantage of the increased draft. Radar

would soon be standard equipment on the lakes, and the war would even spur the development of a new form for the industry's principal bulk cargo. From 1939 to 1945, over half a billion tons of high-grade iron ore were extracted from the Lake Superior ranges. This ore contained an iron content in excess of 51.5 percent and therefore could be dumped into a blast furnace just as it came from the earth. The tremendous wartime demand depleted reserves of this high grade ore at an incredible rate, raising concerns that the supply of ore would soon be exhausted. By 1945, total region reserves were estimated at only 1.2 billion tons; and work was begun in earnest to develop a process to utilize the area's limitless supply of taconite, a low-grade ore that contained less than 35 percent iron. Scientists eventually perfected a method to separate the iron from the unwanted mineral particles by crushing the rock and using magnets to attract the iron, which was then rolled into marble-sized pellets and baked in a furnace to remove moisture. The resulting substance contained over 62 percent iron. Taconite-processing plants were constructed near the mines, and the taconite pellets produced gradually became the primary cargo of the industry in the postwar era.[2]

It seems that the war also brought about a change in the type of individual attracted to life aboard the freighters. After 1945, the nation entered an era of unprecedented growth and prosperity that provided ample opportunities for well-paid blue-collar jobs ashore, with the result that many dependable, family-oriented men left the lakes. One veteran sailor who captained a Pittsburgh boat in the postwar era remembered: "We used to have seamen, you could see them doing all kinds of fancy work and knot work and all that. Wartime came along and all these guys weren't interested in the sea, they just wanted the job. After the war, that's when it went downhill."[3]

While the war did bring significant change to the lakes, perhaps the larger story is one of continuity. In many respects, the Great Lakes bulk cargo industry embarked upon its postwar course without any fundamental change in the basic operating pattern that had existed for decades. The war brought a demand for unprecedented volumes of the traditional bulk cargos; but this was a change in degree, rather than a change in kind. The pooling of vessel dispatch, Sunday and holiday unloading, the lifting of restrictions on Canadian vessel participation, and the limitations on coal and grain cargos were all interim innovations that quickly disappeared with the peace. During the 1946 season—and for decades to follow—the American shippers went back to the routine of moving the bulk cargos up and down the lakes, dependent, once again, on the vagaries of demand for steel products. While technological innovations were employed to modernize the process in the postwar years, no fundamental departure from business as usual was necessary. The LCA continued its highly successful program of benevolent paternalism and frustrated the efforts of the maritime unions for years. In these respects, the industry experience differed from that of many other segments of the nation's economy, which incurred fundamental change as a direct result of the events of the war years.

The wartime experience sounded the final death knell for the package freight segment of Great Lakes shipping. But as we have seen, this development was dictated by competitive realities at work for decades, and the final demise of this industry cannot fairly be viewed as a result of wartime upheaval. Because of gasoline rationing, rubber shortages, and crowded rail service, passenger business on the lakes received a temporary reprieve during the war years; but the car-crazy American public quickly resumed its love affair with the automobile in the postwar era, and the Great Lakes passenger liners gradually disappeared. The extraordinary shipbuilding boom that had fired the local economies of small ports around the lakes would also fade quickly with the coming of peace. In the immediate postwar years, there were few orders for new construction in any of the domestic yards as shippers worldwide absorbed the glut of tonnage produced during the war years. During the 1950s, the American Great Lakes fleet underwent a significant modernization, with the addition of twenty-plus new and larger vessels, most of which were built by American Shipbuilding, the Great Lakes Engineering Works, and, to a lesser extent, Manitowoc and DeFoe. But these companies were competing for local contracts only as the coastal yards again predominated in the construction of oceangoing vessels, both military and civilian.

The role played by big business in America's war effort has been the subject matter of much historical criticism. The heavy industrial segment of the economy has been variously faulted for delaying the changeover to wartime production in 1940 and 1941, resisting the reconversion of 1944 and 1945, excluding the smaller manufacturer from a fair share of the wartime production pie and amassing excess wartime profits. The Great Lakes shipping industry is not an ideal vehicle to use in evaluating these criticisms, since many of the circumstances and peculiarities of the industry defy replication to other areas of the economy. Unlike the automobile or steel industries, Great Lakes shippers did not have to make fundamental changes in their operations to produce essentially different products for wartime use. Their role, in peace or war, was to deliver bulk commodities, regardless of whether the substance ultimately ended up in a Ford coupe or a Sherman tank, so there was no reason for their industry to be involved in issues such as the conversion or reconversion controversies.[4]

Small operators played a significant role in the wartime story on the lakes, for the great demand for all bulk commodities made cargos available for the Dolores Steamship Company's one ship, as well as the seventy-four bottoms of the Pittsburgh Steamship fleet. Nor does the industry appear liable to a charge of accumulating excess profits. Both the cost per ton and the shipping cost per ton of iron ore were regulated by the Office of Price Administration (OPA) during the war years. From 1937 through 1939, a ton of Mesabi Range high-grade iron ore sold for $4.95 and consumers paid shippers an additional eighty cents per ton to deliver it from the head of the lakes to a Lake Erie port. In 1940, the transportation cost dropped to seventy cents per ton but rose again in 1941 to seventy-seven cents and in 1942 to eighty cents, where it was frozen by the OPA. On 26 November 1943, the OPA granted the carriers an 8 percent increase, to 86.4 cents per ton—less than the 10 percent increase sought by the shippers but sufficient to offset rising costs and return the companies to the level of earnings achieved during the 1939–41 base period. Interlake Steamship Company, one of the largest fleets in the industry, reported a net profit of $1,330,584, or $2.96 per share, for the 1942 season, down from $4.10 per share in 1941. The company reported that the decline was due to an increase in operating costs for crew wages, supplies, and insurance. It would seem that the OPA price control policy was effective in limiting the profits of the lake carriers and that the industry did not reap any major economic windfall from the conflict.[5]

While some aspects of the wartime experience on the Great Lakes were unique, the industry did share many other problems and concerns with other segments of the economy, including a shrinking manpower pool, fierce competition for scarce resources and the struggle to carve out relationships with the myriad of new government agencies. But the most important common element between the national business experience and that of the Great Lakes shippers during the war years lies in the ultimate success achieved by each. In the national emergency posed by the war, the New Deal was forced to turn to businessmen for leadership in constructing the war production machine. The same businessmen who had shouldered much of the blame for the failures of the Depression years were now viewed as the heros of the production miracle. A contemporary magazine hailed the appointment of Donald Nelson as WPB director: "When the nation was in deadly peril it called in as a savior a businessman so much like Babbitt that he could have sued the author of that famous work for libel." Geoffrey Perrett claims that "Nelson's appointment was taken as 'poetic justice' for an entire generation of badly wronged American businessmen."[6]

While this romanticized view of businessman as industrial hero is certainly open to serious debate, it is lent some credence by the experience on the Great Lakes. The LCA and company executives provided the experience and expertise needed to enable their particular industry to meet unprecedented goals in a time of dire national emergency, while entrepreneurs like Harry Defoe, Leathem Smith, and Robert Butler converted tiny family businesses into burgeoning enterprises that helped the nation to meet its desperate need for new shipping. The fact that industry self-interest and individual profit were additional motivating factors should not be allowed to diminish the accomplishments of Great Lakes businesses and their contributions to the country's extraordinary production achievements.

Lastly, the significant contribution of the Great Lakes region to the nation's production miracle was the cumulative result of the efforts of thousands of dedicated individuals who, despite shortages, rationing, and unprecedented demand, simply did their jobs as best they could in difficult times. If, as Charles DeGaulle stated, American industrial power was the decisive factor in the outcome of World War II, then these people were frontline soldiers in the decisive theater of that war.

Appendix A

Bulk Commodity Totals, 1905–1945

Year	Iron Ore (Gross Tons)	Soft and Hard Coal (Net Tons)	Various Grain Types (Net Tons)	Stone (Net Tons)	Total (Net Tons)
1905	33,476,904	14,401,199	6,112,859		58,007,070
1906	37,513,589	17,273,718	6,863,068		66,152,006
1907	41,290,709	21,486,927	7,010,937		74,743,458
1908	25,427,094	19,288,098	6,024,493		53,790,938
1909	41,683,599	18,617,396	6,651,245		71,954,272
1910	42,618,758	26,476,068	5,803,514		80,014,591
1911	32,130,411	25,700,104	6,959,465		68,645,629
1912	47,435,771	24,673,210	9,372,252		89,040,063
1913	49,070,478	33,362,379	11,697,160		100,018,464
1914	32,021,897	27,281,228	9,793,850		72,939,603
1915	46,318,804	26,220,000	11,098,815	3,854,106	93,049,981
1916	64,734,198	28,440,483	10,555,975	5,553,927	117,052,686
1917	62,498,901	31,192,613	7,161,716	6,748,801	115,100,399
1918	61,156,732	32,102,022	6,548,680	7,467,776	114,614,018
1919	47,177,395	26,424,068	6,091,703	6,407,285	91,761,238
1920	58,527,226	26,409,710	6,736,348	7,821,980	106,518,531
1921	22,300,726	26,660,652	12,470,405	3,925,705	68,033,575
1922	42,613,184	19,868,925	14,267,020	7,592,137	89,454,848
1923	59,036,074	33,137,028	11,850,446	9,920,422	121,029,004
1924	42,623,572	25,860,515	15,222,787	9,225,624	98,047,327
1925	54,081,298	28,048,538	13,320,346	11,351,948	113,291,886
1926	58,537,855	31,011,290	12,087,316	12,628,244	121,289,502
1927	51,107,136	34,794,291	14,692,536	14,033,376	120,760,195
1928	53,980,874	34,823,002	16,372,098	15,677,551	127,329,348
1929	65,204,600	39,254,578	10,021,099	16,269,612	138,574,441
1930	46,582,982	38,072,060	9,851,229	12,432,628	112,528,857
1931	23,467,786	31,176,359	9,479,640	7,208,946	74,148,865
1932	3,567,985	24,857,369	8,890,409	3,928,840	41,672,761
1933	21,623,898	31,776,654	8,713,127	6,664,629	71,373,176
1934	22,249,600	35,476,575	7,951,145	7,392,218	75,739,490

Bulk Commodity Totals, 1905–1945—*continued*

Year	Iron Ore (Gross Tons)	Soft and Hard Coal (Net Tons)	Various Grain Types (Net Tons)	Stone (Net Tons)	Total (Net T
1935	28,362,368	35,289,135	6,750,261	9,082,155	82,887
1936	44,822,023	44,699,443	7,433,967	12,080,672	114,414
1937	62,598,836	44,318,765	5,829,399	14,429,379	134,688
1938	19,263,011	34,623,287	10,679,125	8,240,768	75,117
1939	45,072,724	40,368,121	11,172,079	12,208,205	114,229
1940	63,712,982	49,319,604	9,644,950	14,893,316	145,216
1941	80,116,360	53,535,365	11,387,480	17,633,448	172,286
1942	92,076,781	52,533,792	8,501,586	18,570,048	182,731
1943	84,404,852	51,969,459	11,810,116	17,339,675	175,652
1944	81,170,538	60,163,330	16,228,880	16,856,279	184,159
1945	75,714,750	55,246,197	18,717,773	16,318,193	175,082

Source: LCA Annual Report, 1945, LCA Collection.

Appendix B

Iron Ore Shipments, 1926–1945

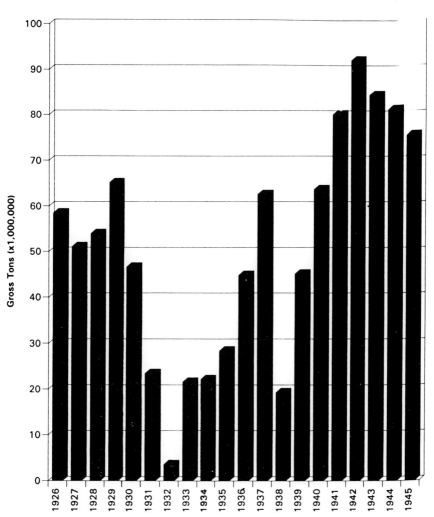

Appendix C

Bulk Commodity Shipments, 1926–1945

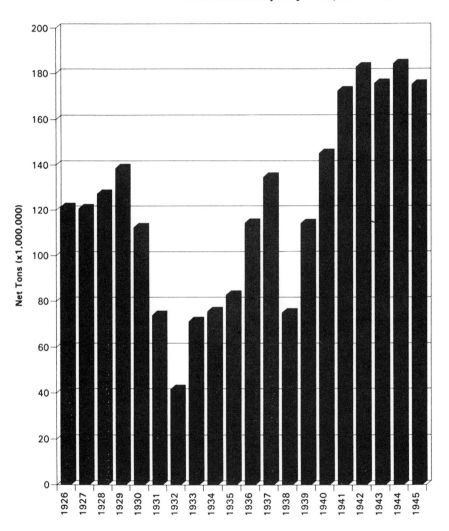

Notes

Notes to Introduction

1. John Morton Blum, *V Was for Victory: Politics and American Culture in World War II* (New York, 1976), 91; Geoffrey Perrett, *Days of Sadness, Years of Triumph: The American People, 1939-1945* (Madison, 1985), 399.
2. Perret, *Days of Sadness*, 261; Jim F. Heath, "Domestic America During World War II: Research Opportunities for Historians," *Journal of American History*, September, 1971, pp. 396-98.
3. Francis Walton, *Miracle of World War II: How American Industry Made Victory Possible* (New York, 1956), 419; WPB, *Steel Expansion for War: A Report of the Steel Division of the War Production Board* (Washington, 1945), 20-21; Douglas A. Fisher, *Steel Serves the Nation: The Fifty Year Story of United States Steel* (Pittsburgh, 1951), 49-50.
4. John P. Morgan, *The Domestic Mining Industry of the United States in World War II* (Washington, 1949), 247.
5. LCA Annual Report, 1945, p. 38; LCA Annual Report 1932, pp. 11, 18.
6. LCA Annual Report, 1932, p. 19.
7. Ibid.

Notes to Chapter 1

1. Samuel Flagg Bemis, *The Diplomacy of the American Revolution* (Bloomington, 1935), 228-238; Maurice G. Baxter, *One and Inseparable: Daniel Webster and the Union* (Cambridge, 1984), 347; Thomas LeDuc, "The Webster–Ashburton Treaty and the Minnesota Iron Ranges," *Journal of American History*, December, 1964, pp. 476-81.
2. *Cleveland Press*, 27 November 1940, IGLR NSC; Jacques Lesstrang, *Cargo Carriers of the Great Lakes* (New York, 1981), 113-17.
3. *Skillings' Mining Review*, 22 September 1945, IGLR NSC; Morgan, *Domestic Mining Industry*, 332-34.
4. International Ship Master's Association of the Great Lakes, *1946 Ship Master's*

Association Directory (New London, Ohio, 1946), 87, 157; Lesstrang, *Cargo Carriers*, 72.

5. Luke Manion, interview, 22 December 1989.
6. Charles P. Larrowe, *Maritime Labor Relations on the Great Lakes* (East Lansing, 1959), 36, 58; Philip Taft, *Organized Labor in American History* (New York, 1964), 199–202.
7. Larrowe, *Maritime Labor Relations*, 40, 53.
8. Luke Manion, interview, 22 December 1989.
9. Morgan, *Domestic Mining Industry*, 333.
10. Lesstrang, *Cargo Carriers*, 117; *Toronto Evening Telegram*, 12 April 1943, IGLR NSC.
11. Morgan, *Domestic Mining Industry*, 334.
12. International Ship Master's Association, *1946 Ship Master's Association Directory*, 159–167.
13. Morgan, *Domestic Mining Industry*, 334.
14. Lesstrang, *Cargo Carriers*, 68, 72.
15. Daniel O. Fletcher, "Package Freighters: Victims of War," *Inland Seas*, Summer 1961, p. 131.
16. "Combat Ships Built on the Great Lakes," *MESR*, September, 1944, p. 187.

Notes to Chapter 2

1. Perrett, *Days of Sadness*, 21; Robert Burns interview, 11 June 1992.
2. LCA Annual Report, 1939, p. 11.
3. *Life*, 19 December 1938, quoted in Richard Ketchum, *The Borrowed Years, 1938–1941* (New York, 1989), 540; LCA Annual Report, 1939, p. 51.
4. Perrett, *Days of Sadness*, 23; LCA Annual Report, 1939, pp. 16–17.
5. *Detroit News*, 24 September 1939, IGLR NSC, LCA Annual Report, 1939, pp. 16–17.
6. "Up and Down the Great Lakes," *MESR*, April 1940, p. 84; *Detroit Free Press*, 19–21 September 1939, IGLR NSC.
7. *Detroit Free Press*, 19–21 September 1939, IGLR NSC. *Cleveland Plain Dealer*, 11 May 1940; *Detroit News*, 17 May 1940.
8. *Detroit News*, 17 May 1940; *Detroit Free Press*, 5–6 and 13 July 1940; *Toledo Blade*, 12 June 1940; *Milwaukee Journal* 5 July 1940; *Cleveland Plain Dealer*, 7 and 12 July 1940.
9. *Detroit Free Press*, 13 July 1940; *Cleveland Plain Dealer*, 19 July 1940; *Detroit News*, 8 and 9 May 1941.
10. Ketchum, *Borrowed Years*, 619–20; *Time*, 30 March 1942, pp. 70–71; A. T. Wood to Ralph Budd, 21 June 1940, LCA Collection.
11. LCA Annual Report, 1940, pp. 43, 53.
12. *Cleveland Plain Dealer*, 19 June and 18 September 1940, IGLR NSC.
13. LCA Annual Report, 1940, p. 16.
14. Val Eichenlaub, *Weather and Climate of the Great Lakes Region* (Notre Dame, 1979), 300–301; *Detroit Free Press*, 12 November 1940, IGLR NSC.

15. John LeCorn, interview, 29 July 1992.
16. LCA Annual Report, 1940, p. 42.
17. Edward Baganz, interview, 5 August 1992.
18. Captain Harold B. McCool, quoted in Eichenlaub, *Weather and Climate*, 300.
19. LCA Annual Report, 1940, pp. 10, 53.
20. Ralph Budd to C. E. Carlson, F. J. Gavin, and A. T. Wood, 17 December 1940, LCA Collection; A. T. Wood to Ralph Budd, 17 December 1940 and A. T. Wood to Ralph Budd, n.d., LCA Collection.
21. James McGregor Burns, *Roosevelt: The Soldier of Freedom* (New York, 1970), 28, 118; Perrett, *Days of Sadness*, 183–85.
22. Perret, *Days of Sadness*, 74; Burns, *Roosevelt*, 51–52.
23. American Iron and Steel Institute, press release 11 October 1940, LCA Collection; Burns, *Roosevelt*, 52; Karl W. Fischer to A. T. Wood, 5 December 1940, LCA Collection; Perrett, *Days of Sadness*, 179.
24. Ralph Budd to C. E. Carlson, F. J. Gavin, and A. T. Wood, 17 December 1940 and Karl W. Fischer to A. T. Wood, 7 December 1940, LCA Collection; LCA Annual Report, 1941, p. 54.
25. Perry Klumph, interview, 14 July 1992.
26. *Toronto Evening Telegram*, 8 May and 21 June 1941 and *Detroit News*, 24 August 1941, IGLR NSC; LCA Annual Report, 1940, p. 9.
27. *Toledo Blade*, 7 October 1941 and *Detroit Free Press*, 8 and 9 October 1941, IGLR NSC; A. T. Wood to Ralph Budd, 3 November 1941, letter and postal telegram, LCA Collection; LCA Annual Report, 1941, pp. 10, 40, 54.
28. "Up and Down the Great Lakes," *MESR*, February, 1941, pp. 91–92, and April 1941, p. 110; Jack Bauer, "Inland Seas and Overseas: Shipbuilding on the Great Lakes During World War II," *Inland Seas*, Summer 1982, p. 84.
29. *MESR*, February, 1941, p. 49; "Up and Down the Great Lakes," *MESR*, April 1941, p. 110.
30. "Up and Down the Great Lakes," *MESR*, April 1941, p. 110.

Notes to Chapter 3

1. Ketchum, *Borrowed Years*, 625; Perrett, *Days of Sadness*, 256; U.S., National Archives and Records Service, *Federal Records of World War II*, vol. 1 (Washington, 1950), 305, 331.
2. Joseph B. Eastman to A. T. Wood, 16 April 1942, LCA Collection.
3. A. T. Wood to Great Lakes Vessel Operators, 21 April 1942, LCA Collection; Lake Vessel Committee to Robert D. Smith, 13 April 1943, LCA Collection; LCA Annual Report, 1942, p. 10.
4. "Estimated Ore Movement, Great Lakes Fleet, Season 1942," LCA Collection; *Detroit News*, 19 July 1942, LCA NSC; Joseph B. Eastman to A. T. Wood, 16 April 1942, LCA Collection; U.S., Office of Defense Transportation, *Civilian War Transport: A Record of the Control of Domestic Traffic Operations, 1941–1946* (Washington, 1948), 180.

5. U.S., Office of Defense Transportation, *Civilian War Transport*, 180–81; "Proposed Sale of Sixteen Ore-Carrying Vessels By U.S. Maritime Commission," n.d., WMC.
6. Karl W. Fischer to A. D. Whitehead, 15 July 1941, WPD, RG 165; F. R. Russell to W. Y. Elliott, 30 March 1942, WPD, RG 165; C. E. Adams to J. S. Knowlson, 9 May 1942, WPD, RG 165.
7. LCA Annual Report, 1942, pp. 15–16, 50; *Detroit Free Press*, 7 April 1942, IGLR NSC.
8. U.S. Office of Defense Transportation, *Civilian War Transport*, 181.
9. Clarence McTevia, interview, 22 July 1992.
10. LCA Annual Report, 1942, pp. 12, 16.
11. *Detroit Free Press*, 3 December 1942, IGLR NSC. LCA Annual Report, 1942, p. 40.
12. Fletcher, "Package Freighters," 132, 135; LCA Annual Report, 1942, p. 42.
13. *Detroit News*, 14 March 1942, IGLR NSC; Brian Higgins, "Fresh Water Flat Tops," *Inland Seas*, Summer 1978, 103–12; Sharon E. McHaney, "Michigan Goes to War," *Michigan History*, November/December 1992, 22.
14. *Detroit Free Press*, 8 June and 13 July 1941, IGLR NSC.
15. *Detroit Free Press* 2 and 16 June 1943, and 4 April 1944; *Cleveland Press*, 15 June 1944, IGLR NSC.
16. Perrett, *Days of Sadness*, 258; Burns, *Roosevelt*, 333–34; "Up and Down the Great Lakes," *MESR*, January, 1943, p. 174.
17. LCA Annual Report, 1943, pp. 12–13, 56, 58; *St. Ignace Republican-News*, 1 April 1943, IGLR NSC.
18. LVC Minutes, 19 April 1943, LCA Collection; *Detroit Free Press*, 22 April 1943, IGLR NSC; LVC Minutes, 4 May 1943, LCA Collection.
19. LVC Minutes, 14 May 1943, LCA Collection. For an interesting discussion of the significance of "feasibility" in the war production program, see John E. Brigante, *The Feasibility Dispute: Determination of War Production Objectives for 1942 and 1943* (Washington, 1950).
20. LVC Minutes, 19 May and 2 June 1943, LCA Collection.
21. *Detroit Free Press*, 2 and 3 June 1943, IGLR NSC. McTevia, interview, 22 July 1992; *Detroit Free Press*, 16 and 17 June 1943 and *St Ignace Republican-News*, 17 June 1943, IGLR NSC.
22. LVC Minutes, 2 June 1943, LCA Collection; K. H. Suder to Iron-ore Customers, 15 June 1943, LCA Collection; LVC Minutes, 1 July 1943, LCA Collection; H. Van B. Cleveland to Karl Suder, 3 July 1943, LCA Collection.
23. Master Sheet for *Lake Fresco*, IGLR "Vessel File;" *Manitowoc Herald-Times*, 18 June 1943, and *Detroit News*, 19 June 1943, IGLR NSC.
24. *Detroit News*, 6 June and 15 July 1943; *Detroit Free Press*, 28 July and 30 September 1943; *Toledo Blade*, 13 October 1943; *Wall Street Journal*, 18 October 1943; IGLR NSC. LVC Minutes, 3 August 1943, LCA Collection.
25. John LeCorn, interview, 29 July 1992.
26. U.S., Office of Defense Transportation, *Civilian War Transport*, 181–82; LCA Annual Report, 1943, p. 56.

27. LCA Annual Report, 1943, pp. 11, 56; "Up and Down the Great Lakes," *MESR*, March 1944, p. 214.

28. Perrett, *Days of Sadness*, 301, 398.

29. LVC Minutes, 2 May 1944, LCA Collection; LCA Annual Report, 1944, pp. 47–48.

30. *Detroit Free Press*, 28 April 1944, IGLR NSC; "Estimate of the Capacity of the U.S. Registry Great Lakes [*sic*] for the 1944 Navigation Season," WPB, RG 179; *Toledo Blade*, 13 May 1944, IGLR NSC; LCA Annual Report, 1944, pp. 10, 12, 48.

31. LVC Minutes, 2 March and 9 May 1945, LCA Collection.

32. LCA Annual Report, 1945, pp. 12, 15, 17, 38, 51; *Skilling's Mining Review*, 2 June 1945, IGLR NSC.

33. LVC Minutes, 23 August 1945, LCA Collection; LCA Annual Report, 1945, p. 10.

34. Kathleen Warnes, "The Submarines for World War II," *Inland Seas*, Spring 1986, p. 14; Leathem D. Smith, "War Shipbuilding on the Great Lakes," *Inland Seas*, Spring 1946, pp. 147–48; "Up and Down the Great Lakes," *MESR*, February, 1942, p. 122.

35. Smith, "War Shipbuilding," 147; *Bay City Times*, 30 April 1944, IGLR NSC; Bauer, "Inland Seas and Overseas," 166.

36. Smith, "War Shipbuilding," 148–150; *Green Bay Press Gazette*, 29 December 1944, IGLR NSC.

37. *Green Bay Press Gazette*, 29 December 1944, IGLR NSC.

38. Smith, "War Shipbuilding," 148; "Maritime Commission C1-M-AV1 Cargo Ships Built on Great Lakes," *MESR*, December 1942, p. 202.

39. *Milwaukee Journal*, 5 May 1943; *Detroit News*, 8 May 1943; *Detroit Free Press*, 10 May 1943; and *Lima News* (Ohio), 6 May 1943—all in IGLR NSC.

40. Smith, "War Shipbuilding," 148.

41. *Algonac Courier* (Michigan), 18 June 1942, p. 1; Jeffrey L. Rodengen, *The Legend of Chris-Craft* (Ft. Lauderdale, 1988), 128, 136; Bauer, "Inland Seas and Overseas," 170; *Detroit Free Press*, 27 August and 15 September 1940 and 7 January 1942, IGLR NSC.

42. Bauer, "Inland Seas and Overseas," 170; "Up and Down the Great Lakes," *MESR*, March 1945, p. 190.

Notes to Chapter 4

1. "Resolution," 1 August 1940, LCA Collection.

2. *Cleveland Plain Dealer*, 13 August 1940, IGLR NSC.

3. "Special Precautions To Be Taken on Shipboard," 1 August 1940, LCA Collection.

4. Logbooks of the Steamers *Carmi A. Thompson* (1942–47) and *Champlain* (1944–45), IGLR; In addition to the logbooks specifically mentioned, logbooks of the tug *William A. Whitney* and the steamers *Standard Portland Cement, Lackawanna*, and *Charles Hubbard* were also examined.

5. Perry Klumph, interview, 14 July 1992; Edward Baganz, interview, 5 August 1922.
6. "Meeting of Vessel and Dock Operators," 12 July 1940, LCA Collection.
7. *Toledo Blade*, 26 August 1939; *Detroit Free Press*, 3 and 4 September 1939; and *Cleveland Plain Dealer*, 12 October 1939.—all in IGLR NSC.
8. *Detroit Free Press*, 16 June, 3 and 12 August 1940, IGLR NSC; "Circular No. 1258," A. T. Wood to Members, 9 September 1940, LCA Collection.
9. *Detroit Free Press*, 4 August 1940 and 11 and 16 February 1941 and *Toledo Blade*, 28 June 1941, IGLR NSC.
10. A. T. Wood to August M. Krech, 16 December 1941, LCA Collection; A. M. Krech to A. T. Wood, 23 December 1941, LCA Collection; A. T. Wood to Commanding General, Sixth Corps Area, 29 December 1941, LCA Collection.
11. William B. Stewart to A. T. Wood, 29 December 1941, LCA Collection; A. C. Sullivan to A. T. Wood, 8 January 1942, LCA Collection; A. T. Wood to Henry L. Stimson, 19 January 1942, LCA Collection.
12. Major General E. S. Adams to A. T. Wood, 28 January 1942, LCA Collection.
13. LCA Counsel to the Honorable Prentiss M. Brown, 30 January 1942, LCA Collection; Major General J. M. Cummins to A. T. Wood, 3 February 1942, and A. T. Wood to Joseph Eastman, 27 February 1942, LCA Collection.
14. Colonel C. P. Gross to Joseph Eastman, 5 March 1942, LCA Collection; A. T. Wood to A. H. Ferbert, 6 March 1942, LCA Collection.
15. Memorandum, Commandant, Ninth Naval District to Chief of Naval Operations, 19 January 1942, WPD, RG 165; Memorandum, G-2 to Chief of Staff, 11 February 1942, WPD, RG 165; Memorandum for Chief of Staff, 7 February 1942, WPD, RG 165; Memorandums to Chief of Engineers, Chief of Army Air Forces, and Chief of Infantry, 15–16 February 1942, WPD, RG 165.
16. Memorandum from Assistant Chief of the Air Staff to Assistant Chief of Staff, 21 February 1942, WPD, RG 165.
17. Ibid.; "Proceedings of Board of Officers for Investigation of Protection of Sault Ste. Marie Locks," 25 February 1942, WPD, RG 165; Memorandum to the Chief of Staff, "Re: Report of Inspection of Defense Measures at the Sault Ste. Marie Locks and Canal Area," 6 March 1942, OPD, RG 165.
18. Memorandum for the Chief of Staff, 18 February 1942, WPD, RG 165; Major General J. M. Cummins to A. T. Wood, 21 March 1942, and Sault Ste. Marie Military District Operations Order No. 1, 28 March 1942, LCA Collection; *Detroit Free Press*, 24 March 1943 and 24 March 1946, IGLR NSC; Paul T. Hurt, Jr., "Vacation Voyages on the Inland Seas," *Inland Seas*, Winter 1951, p. 258.
19. Memorandum, Major W. F. Train to Assistant Chief of Staff, 11 July 1942, OPD, RG 165.
20. *Sault Ste. Marie Evening News*, 27 May 1942.
21. Train, Memorandum, 11 July 1942.
22. *Sault Ste. Marie Evening News*, 1 September and 18 December 1942.
23. *Sault Ste. Marie Evening News* , 6 April 1942; Milton Ward and Stanley Bush, telephone interviews, 10 September 1992.

24. *Sault Ste. Marie Evening News*, 27 May, 22 August, and 15 October 1942.
25. "Sault Ste. Marie Military District," RG 338; *Sault Ste. Marie Evening News*, 15 July 1943.
26. Major General V. I. Peterson to Chief of Staff, 6 March 1942, OPD, RG 165; "Note for the Record," 14 July 1942, OPD, RG 165; Memorandum for the Adjutant General, 16 April 1942, OPD, RG 165.
27. Perry Klumph, interview, 14 July 1992.
28. Memorandum for the Chief of Staff, "Re: Garrison at Sault Ste. Marie," 14 March 1944, OPD, RG 165.
29. J. Edgar Hoover to A. T. Wood, 29 December 1941, LCA Collection.
30. Ibid.; "Resolution," 1 August 1940, LCA Collection; "Circular No. 1351," 12 March 1942, LCA Collection.
31. U.S. Coast Guard, *The Coast Guard at War*, vol. 19, *Port Security* (Washington, 1949), 8, 13–14.
32. Ibid., 22–23, 43.
33. Note for the Record, 21 August 1942, OPD, RG 165.
34. *Detroit News*, 13 July 1942, IGLR NSC. Clarence McTevia, interview, 22 July 1992; Luke Manion, interview, 22 December 1989.
35. Clarence McTevia, interview, 22 July 1992.
36. U.S. Civilian Production Administration, *Minutes of the War Production Board: January 20, 1942 to October 9, 1945* (Washington, 1946), 112; *Vermilion News* (Ohio), 9 April 1942 and *Detroit Free Press*, 15 May 1942, IGLR NSC.
37. *Detroit Free Press*, 16 May 1942 and 27 June and 4 July 1943, IGLR NSC.
38. *Detroit News*, 14 December 1941, IGLR NSC; Theodore F. Koop, *Weapon of Silence* (Chicago, 1946), 168; *Detroit Free Press*, 11 March 1942, IGLR NSC.
39. A. T. Wood to Rear Admiral H. L. Vickery, 17 March 1942, and H. L. Vickery to A. T. Wood, 31 March 1942, LCA Collection; A. T. Wood to Hugh Kane (managing editor, *Cleveland News*), 3 April 1942, LCA Collection; Paul Bellamy to A. T. Wood, 6 April 1942, LCA Collection.
40. Richard Gid Powers, *Secrecy and Power: The Life of J. Edgar Hoover* (New York, 1987), 255.

Notes to Chapter 5

1. *Detroit Free Press*, 12 May 1940, IGLR NSC.
2. "Memorandum Concerning Deferment of Great Lakes Seamen," n.d., LCA Collection; Perrett, *Days of Sadness*, 40; U.S. Selective Service System, *Industrial Deferment: Special Monograph No. 6* (Washington, 1948), 3.
3. U.S., Selective Service System, *Industrial Deferment*, 79; *Toronto Evening Telegram*, 11 February 1941, IGLR NSC; "Memorandum Concerning Deferment of Great Lakes Seamen," n.d., LCA Collection.
4. "Memorandum Concerning Deferment of Great Lakes Seamen," n.d., LCA Collection.
5. *Toledo Blade*, 8 June 1943, IGLR NSC.

6. War Department Memorandum, "Use of Prisoners on Great Lakes Ore Vessels," WPB, RG 179; Memorandum, J. T. Whiting to H. G. Batcheller, 25 August 1943, WPB, RG 179; *Detroit Free Press*, 21 August 1943, IGLR NSC.

7. Albert A. Blum, *Drafted or Deferred: Practices Past and Present* (Ann Arbor, 1967), 126–27.

8. Ibid., 132–33, 137.

9. "Proposed Manpower Program for the Great Lakes Prepared by the Recruitment and Manning Organization of the War Shipping Administration," n.d., LCA Collection; "Statement of D. C. Potts, Manager of Traffic, Pittsburgh Steamship Company," n.d., LCA Collection.

10. Larrowe, *Maritime Labor Relation*, 58–62.

11. Ibid., 56–57; *In re* Pittsburgh Steamship Co. and NMU of America (CIO) 69 NLRB 1395, 1414 (1946).

12. Larrowe, *Maritime Labor Relations*, 63; *In re* Pittsburgh Steamship Co. and NMU of America (CIO) 69 NLRB 1395, 1399, 1402–11.

13. Memorandum, "Manpower Problem on the Great Lakes," Milton Starr to Samuel Hassman, 28 February 1944, WPB, RG 179; Larrowe, *Maritime Labor Relations*, 62.

14. "Program for Manning Great Lakes Ships Transporting Iron Ore, Coal, Limestone, and Grain," n.d., LCA Collection; *Toledo Blade*, 6 March 1944, IGLR NSC; Karl H. Suder to Lake Vessel Operators, 25 March 1944, LCA Collection; Telegram, 23 March 1944, LCA Collection.

15. Marshall B. Dimock to Otto Beyer, 25 March 1944, LCA Collection; W. Y. Elliott to Colonel E. F. Jeffe, 25 March 1944, WPB, RG 179.

16. "Revised and Enlarged Program for Manning All Great Lakes Ships," 4 April 1944, LCA Collection.

17. *Toledo Blade*, 8 March 1944, and *Detroit Free Press*, 15 March 1944, IGLR NSC; LCA Scrapbook, 1 November 1942–10 October 1944, 11 April 1944; Blum, *Drafted or Deferred*, 133; *Detroit Free Press*, 12 April 1944, IGLR NSC.

18. "Office of Defense Transportation (ODT-540)," 19 April 1944, LCA Collection; "Report of Manpower Sub-Committee of Lake Vessel Committee," 1 July 1944, LCA Collection; LCA Annual Report, 1944, p. 10.

19. Karl H. Suder to E. J. Connors, 16 November 1944, LCA Collection; "Report of Manpower Sub-Committee of Lake Vessel Committee," December 1944, LCA Collection.

20. "Up and Down the Great Lakes," *MESR*, December 1944, p. 204; "Recruitment of Experienced Lake Seamen for Ocean Shipping Jobs," 1 December 1944, LCA Collection; LVC Minutes, 31 January 1945, LCA Collection.

21. Blum, *Drafted or Deferred*, 141, 149.

22. J. M. Johnson to Employers in the Inland Waterways and Great Lakes Industry, 17 February 1945, LCA Collection; J. M. Johnson to Paul V. McNutt, 6 March 1945, LCA Collection.

23. U.S. Civilian Production Administration, *Minutes of the War Production Board*, 392; *Detroit Free Press*, 17 March 1945, IGLR NSC; LVC Minutes, 19 March 1945, LCA Collection.

24. "Up and Down the Great Lakes," *MESR*, March 1945, p. 194, and June 1945, p. 186; Douglas E. Wilson to Oliver Burnham, 24 April 1945, LCA Collection; Blum, *Drafted or Deferred*, 156.
25. Clarence McTevia, interview, 22 July 1992; Perry Klumph, interview, 14 July 1992; Hubert Kessel, interview, 17 June 1992.
26. Clarence McTevia, interview, 22 July 1992.

Notes to Chapter 6

1. Perrett, *Days of Sadness*, 84.
2. *Detroit Free Press*, 4 August 1940, and *Detroit News*, 9 March 1942, IGLR NSC; H. W. Garner to D. M. Nelson, 11 April 1942, LCA Collection.
3. *Milwaukee Journal*, 7 October 1941, IGLR NSC; L. C. Sabin to R. G. Barrows, 24 February 1941, LCA Collection; Lesstrang, *Cargo Carriers*, 93–94.
4. L. C. Sabin to R. G. Barrow, 24 February 1941, LCA Collection.
5. A. T. Wood to Ralph Budd, 10 October 1941 and A. T. Wood to Prentiss M. Brown, 8 December 1941, LCA Collection; *Detroit Free Press*, 25 February 1942; *Milwaukee Journal*, 2 July 1943; and *Detroit Free Press*, 22 June 1943—all in IGLR NSC.
6. Memorandum, F. R. Stettinius, Jr., to W. L. Batt, Jr., 8 January 1941, and "Confidential Memorandum, Sault Ste. Marie, Michigan," 12 December 1940, WPB, RG 179.
7. Memorandum, "Re: Ore Movement for the St. Mary's Falls Canals, Michigan," and Accompanying Teletype Message, 9 March 1942, OPD, RG 165.
8. *Detroit Free Press*, 9 March and 2 June 1942, IGLR NSC.
9. U.S. Civilian Production Administration, *Minutes of the War Production Board*, 111–12.
10. Jesse Jones to Donald Nelson, 31 August 1942, WPB, RG 179; Committee Report to Donald Nelson, 18 September 1942, WPB, RG 179.
11. Memorandum, G. E. Textor to F. Eberstadt, 14 October 1942, WPB, RG 179; A. F. Shafter to Donald M. Nelson, 9 November 1942, WPB, RG 179.
12. *Detroit Free Press*, ca. 8 August 1942, IGLR NSC; E. A. Locke, Jr., to Hugh A. Fulton, 30 April 1943, WPB, RG 179; *Inside Michigan*, August 1952, p. 28; Frank P. Erichsen, "Escanaba Ore Docks Construction Project: October 1942 to June 1943," Escanaba Public Library, Escanaba, Michigan.
13. "Resume of Escanaba Project," 23 April 1943, WPB, RG 179; Morgan, *Domestic Mining Industry*, 332; Erichsen, "Escanaba Ore Docks," 3; *Detroit Free Press*, 14 April 1943, and *Toronto Evening Telegram*, 20 November 1944, IGLR NSC.
14. *Skilling's Mining Review*, 30 June 1945; *St. Ignace Republican-News*, 26 December 1946; and *Detroit Free Press*, 14 April 1943—IGLR NSC; A. A. Imberman, *Baltimore Sun* "Hush-Hush on the Escanaba Project," March 23, 1943, file 633.11, WPB, RG 179; Ralph Budd to C. E. Carlson, F. J. Gavin, and A. T. Wood, 17 December 1940, LCA Collection; Minutes of LCA Meeting, 21 December 1940, LCA Collection.

15. *Cleveland Press*, 20 February 1942; *Detroit Free Press*, 21 February 1942; and *Duluth News-Tribune*, 11 June 1944—all in IGLR NSC; Jacques Lesstrang, *Seaway* (Seattle, 1976), 150–51.
16. *Duluth News-Tribune*, 11 June 1944, IGLR NSC.
17. LCA Annual Report, 1944, pp. 15–16; Harry C. Brockel, "World War II Secrets of Lake Michigan," *Inland Seas*, Summer 1978, pp. 107–9.
18. Charles H. Coleman, *Shipbuilding Activities of the National Defense Advisory Commission and Office of Production Management, July 1940 to December 1941* (Washington, 1945), 22–23; 49 Stat 1985.
19. 53 Stat 1183; 54 Stat 1106.
20. "Up and Down the Great Lakes," *MESR*, April 1941, p. 108; David Buchanan, telephone interview, 5 November 1989.
21. *Detroit Free Press*, 12 August 1941, IGLR NSC; *Chicago Journal of Commerce*, 13 September 1941, p. 15; John Horton, telephone interview, 5 November 1989.
22. E. S. Land to A. T. Wood, 5 September 1941, WM Collection.
23. Ira L. Ewers to A. T. Wood, 26 September 1941, WM Collection.
24. U.S. Maritime Commission Minutes, 8, 11, and 14 October 1941; "Proposed Sale of Sixteen Ore-carrying Vessels by U.S. Maritime Commission," n.d., WM Collection.
25. Ira Ewers to A. T. Wood, 11 October 1941, WM Collection; Lindsay C. Warren (U.S. comptroller general) to Admiral Land (U.S. Maritime Commission), 17 February 1943, WM Collection.
26. "Statement of Cost and Valuation as of May 6, 1943—Date of Delivery," n.d., WM Collection; "Contract Between U.S. Maritime Commission and Wilson Transit Company," 26 April 1943, WM Collection; "Proposed Sale of Sixteen Ore-carrying Vessels by U.S. Maritime Commission," n.d., WM Collection; "Vessel Operating Statements for the Period Ending December 31, 1943," n.d., WM Collection.
27. Walton, *Miracle of World War II*, 419.

Notes to Conclusion

1. Perrett, *Days of Sadness*, 353, 401, 403.
2. *Detroit Free Press*, 7 October 1945, IGLR NSC; Lesstrang, *Cargo Carriers*, 113.
3. Perry Klumph, interview, 14 July 1992.
4. For a list of some of the sources dealing with these issues, see Jim Heath, "Domestic America During World War II: Research Opportunities for Historians," *Journal of American History*, September 1971, pp. 384–414.
5. *Cleveland Plain Dealer*, 18 April 1940, IGLR NSC; LCA Scrapbook, 5 and 8 April 1942 and 28 November 1943; "Up and Down the Great Lakes," *MESR*, May 1943, p. 230.
6. *Life*, 6 July 1942, quoted in Perrett, *Days of Sadness*, 256.

Bibliography

Much of the research for this work was completed at the Institute for Great Lakes Research, Bowling Green State University, Perrysburg, Ohio. Of particular importance was the Lake Carriers Association Collection, which was still "unprocessed" at the time this research was completed in 1991. Most of the LCA material utilized here can be found in the National Defense files (box 32), Lake Vessel Committee files (boxes 42, 75), Minutes of Meetings file (box 75), WPB file (box 75), and several miscellaneous files in box 75A.

The institute also maintains a collection of several hundred ring binders containing newspaper clippings from cities around the Great Lakes. The binders are arranged in chronological order and offer the researcher a wonderfully efficient tool for reviewing a particular time period.

Books

Bailey, Thomas A. *A Diplomatic History of the American People.* 7th ed. New York: Meredith, 1964.

Baxter, Maurice G. *One and Inseparable: Daniel Webster and the Union.* Cambridge, Mass.: Harvard University Press, 1984.

Bemis, Samuel Flagg. *The Diplomacy of the American Revolution.* Bloomington: Indiana University Press, 1957.

Blum, Albert. *Drafted or Deferred: Practices Past and Present.* Ann Arbor: University of Michigan Press, 1967.

Blum, John Morton. *V Was for Victory.* New York: Harcourt Brace Jovanovich, 1976.

Bowen, Dana Thomas. *Lore of the Lakes.* Cleveland: Freshwater, 1940.

———. *Memories of the Lakes.* Cleveland: Freshwater, 1946.

Brigante, John E. *The Feasibility Dispute: Determination of War Production Objectives for 1942 and 1943.* Washington: GPO 1950.

Brinkley, David. *Washington Goes to War.* New York: Knopf, 1988.

Burns, James MacGregor. *Roosevelt: The Soldier of Freedom.* New York: Harcourt Brace Jovanovich, 1970.

Catton, Bruce. *The War Lords of Washington.* New York: Harcourt, Brace, 1948.

Coleman, Charles H. *Shipbuilding Activities of the National Defense Advisory Commission and Office of Production Management, July, 1940 to December, 1941.* Washington: Civilian Production Administration, 1946.

Conn, Stetson, Rose C. Engelman, and Byron Fairchild. *Guarding the United States and Its Outposts.* Washington: GPO 1964.

Eichenlaub, Val. *Weather and Climate of the Great Lakes Region.* Notre Dame, Indiana: University of Notre Dame Press, 1979.

Farago, Ladislas. *The Game of the Foxes.* New York: David McKay, 1971.

Fisher, Douglas A. *Steel Serves the Nation, 1901-1951: The Fifty Year Story of United States Steel.* Pittsburgh: U.S. Steel, 1951.

International Ship Masters Association of the Great Lakes. *1946 Ship Masters Association Directory.* New London, Ohio: International Ship Masters Association of the Great Lakes.

Janeway, Eliot. *The Struggle for Survival: A Chronicle of Economic Mobilization in World War II.* New Haven: Yale University Press, 1951.

Kaplan, A. D. H. *The Liquidation of War Production: Cancellation of War Contracts and Disposal of Government Owned Plants and Surpluses.* New York: McGraw-Hill, 1944.

Kennett, Lee. *For the Duration: The United States Goes to War, Pearl Harbor-1942.* New York: Charles Scribner's Sons, 1985.

Ketchum, Richard M. *The Borrowed Years, 1938-1941.* New York: Random House, 1989.

Klingaman, William K. *1941: Our Lives in a World on the Edge.* New York: Harper & Row, 1988.

Koop, Theodore F. *Weapon of Silence.* Chicago: University of Chicago Press, 1946.

Lake Carriers Association. Annual Reports, 1939-45. Cleveland: Lake Carriers Association.

Lane, Frederic C. *Ships for Victory: A History of Shipbuilding under the U.S. Maritime Commission In World War II.* Baltimore: Johns Hopkins University Press, 1951.

Larrowe, Charles P. *Maritime Labor Relations on the Great Lakes.* East Lansing: Michigan State University, Labor and Industrial Relations Center, 1959.

Lesstrang, Jacques. *Cargo Carriers of the Great Lakes.* New York: American Legacy, 1977.

———. *Seaway.* Seattle: Salisbury, 1976.

Morgan, John P. *The Domestic Mining Industry of the United States In World War II.* Washington: GPO 1949.

Nelson, Donald M. *Arsenal of Democracy: The Story of American War Production.* New York: Harcourt, Brace, 1946.

Perrett, Geoffrey. *Days of Sadness, Years of Triumph: The American People, 1939-1945.* Madison: University of Wisconsin Press, 1973.

Polenberg, Richard, ed. *America at War: The Home Front, 1941-1945.* Englewood Cliffs, NJ: Prentice-Hall, 1968.

Powers, Richard Gid. *Secrecy and Power: The Life of J. Edgar Hoover.* New York: Free Press, 1987.

Rauch, Basil. *Roosevelt: From Munich to Pearl Harbor.* New York: Creative Age, 1950.

Rodengen, Jeffrey L. *The Legend of Chris-Craft.* Fort Lauderdale, Florida: Write Stuff Syndicate, 1988.

Rose, Joseph R. *American Wartime Transportation.* New York: Thomas Y. Crowell, 1953.

Taft, Philip. *Organized Labor in American History.* New York: Harper & Row, 1964.

Terkel, Studs. *The Good War: An Oral History of World War II.* New York: Pantheon Books, 1984.

United States Civilian Production Administration. *Industrial Mobilization for War, History of the War Production Board and Predecessor Agencies, 1940–45.* Vol. 1, *Program and Administration.* Washington: Civilian Production Administration 1947.

———. *Minutes of the War Production Board: January 20, 1942 to October 9, 1945.* Washington: Civilian Production Administration 1946.

United States Coast Guard. *The Coast Guard at War.* Vol. 18, *Port Security.* Washington: U.S. Coast Guard Public Information Division, 1949.

———. *The Coast Guard at War.* Vol. 19, *Auxiliary.* Washington: U.S. Coast Guard Public Information Division, 1949.

United States National Archives and Records Service. *Federal Records of World War II.* Washington: National Archives and Records Service, 1950.

United States Office of Defense Transportation. *Civilian War Transport: A Record of the Controls of Domestic Traffic Operations, 1941–46.* Washington: Office of Defense Transportation, 1948.

United States Selective Service System. *Industrial Deferment: Special Monograph No. 6.* Washington: Selective Service Administration, 1948.

United States War Production Board. *Steel Expansion for War: A Report of the Steel Division of the War Production Board.* Washington: War Production Board 1945.

Walton, Francis. *Miracle of World War II: The Story of American War Production.* New York: Macmillan, 1956.

Weintraub, Stanley. *Long Day's Journey into War.* New York: Truman Talley Books, 1991.

Wilson, G. Lloyd, ed. *Selected Papers and Addresses of Joseph B. Eastman, Director, Office of Defense Transportation, 1942–1944.* New York: Simmons–Boardman, 1948.

Wright, Richard J. *Freshwater Whales: A History of the American Shipbuilding Company and Its Predecessors.* Kent State University Press, 1969.

Periodicals

Bauer, K. Jack. "Inland Seas and Overseas: Shipbuilding on the Great Lakes During World War II." *Inland Seas* 38(1982): 84–94, 165–170.

Brockel, Harry C. "World War II Secrets of Lake Michigan." *Inland Seas* 34(Summer 1978): 103–12.

Fletcher, Daniel O. "Package Freighters: Victims of War." *Inland Seas* 17(Summer 1961): 131–42.

Heath, Jim F. "Domestic America During World War II: Research Opportunities for Historians." *Journal of American History* 63(September 1971): 384–414.

Higgins, Brian. "Fresh Water Flat Tops." *Inland Seas* 43(Winter 1987): 264–69.

Hurt, Paul T., Jr. "Vacation Voyages on the Great Lakes." *Inland Seas* 7(Winter 1951): 203–8.

Inland Seas. (Great Lakes Historical Society) 1–45(1945–89).

Inside Michigan (August 1952): 26–28.

LeDuc, Thomas. "The Webster-Ashburton Treaty and the Minnesota Iron Ranges." *Journal of American History* 51(December 1964): 476–481.

Marine Engineering and Shipping Review 44–50 (1939–45).

Smith, Leathem D. "War Shipbuilding on the Great Lakes." *Inland Seas* 2 (Spring 1946): 147–54.

Time (30 March 1942): 70–71.

Warnes, Kathleen. "The Submarines for World War II." *Inland Seas* 42(Spring 1986): 12–23.

Unpublished Material

Clive, Alan Gale. "The Society and Economy of Wartime Michigan, 1939–1945." Ph.D. diss., University of Michigan, 1976.

Erichsen, Frank P. "Escanaba Ore Docks Construction Project: October, 1942 to June, 1943." Escanaba Public Library, Escanaba, Michigan.

Lake Carriers Association. Newspaper Scrapbook. Institute for Great Lakes Research, Bowling Green State University.

Lake Carriers Association Collection. Institute for Great Lakes Research, Bowling Green State University.

Logbook of the Steamer *Carmi A. Thompson*, 1942–47. Institute for Great Lakes Research, Bowling Green State University.

Logbook of the Steamer *Champlain*, 1944–45. Institute for Great Lakes Research, Bowling Green State University.

Logbook of the steamer *Charles Hubbard*, 1941. Institute for Great Lakes Research, Bowling Green State University.

Logbook of the Steamer *Lackawanna*, 1942. Institute for Great Lakes Research, Bowling Green State University.

Logbook of the Steamer *Standard Portland Cement*, 1945. Institute for Great Lakes Research, Bowling Green State University.

Logbook of the Tug *William A. Whitney*, 1941–42. Institute for Great Lakes Research, Bowling Green State University.

Newspaper Scrapbook Collection. 1939–46, 40 vols. Institute for Great Lakes Research, Bowling Green State University.

Sault Ste. Marie Military District, Record Group 338, National Archives, Suitland Records Center.
United States Maritime Administration, U.S. Maritime Commission Minutes, 1940–45, Maritime Administration, Washington.
War Plans Division, Record Group 165, National Archives.
War Production Board, Record Group 179, National Archives.
Wilson Marine Collection, Institute for Great Lakes Research, Bowling Green State University.

Personal Interviews

Edward Baganz, personal interview, 5 August 1992, Grosse Pointe Park, Michigan.
David Buchanan, telephone interview, 5 November 1989, Cleveland, Ohio.
Robert S. Burns, personal interview, 11 June 1992, Marine City, Michigan.
Stanley Bush, telephone interview, 10 September 1992, Algiers, Louisiana.
Erik Hirsimaki, telephone interview, 14 March 1990, North Olmsead, Ohio.
John Horton, telephone interview, 5 November 1989, Cleveland, Ohio.
Hubert Kessel, personal interview, 17 June 1992, Marine City, Michigan.
Perry Klumph, personal interview, 14 July 1992, Marine City, Michigan.
John LeCorn, personal interview, 29 July 1992, Marine City, Michigan.
Luke Manion, personal interview, 22 December 1989, Marine City, Michigan.
Clarence McTevia, personal interview, 22 July 1992, Marine City, Michigan.
Glen Nekvasil, telephone interview, 4 November 1989, Cleveland, Ohio.
James Sharrow, telephone interview, 3 November 1989, Duluth, Minnesota.

Index

Titles in the Great Lakes Books Series

LET THE DRUM BEAT: A History of the Detroit Light Guard, *by Stanley D. Solvick, 1988*

AN AFTERNOON IN WATERLOO PARK, *by Gerald Dumas, 1988 (reprint)*

CONTEMPORARY MICHIGAN POETRY: Poems from the Third Coast, *edited by Michael Delp, Conrad Hilberry, and Herbert Scott, 1988*

OVER THE GRAVES OF HORSES, *by Michael Delp, 1988*

WOLF IN SHEEP'S CLOTHING: The Search for a Child Killer, *by Tommy McIntyre, 198*

COPPER-TOED BOOTS, *by Marguerite de Angeli, 1989 (reprint)*

DETROIT IMAGES: Photographs of the Renaissance City, *edited by John J. Bukowczyk and Douglas Aikenhead, with Peter Slavcheff, 1989*

HANGDOG REEF: Poems Sailing the Great Lakes, *by Stephen Tudor, 1989*

DETROIT: City of Race and Class Violence, *revised edition, by B. J. Widick, 1989*

DEEP WOODS FRONTIER: A History of Logging in Northern Michigan, *by Theodore J. Karamanski, 1989*

ORVIE, THE DICTATOR OF DEARBORN, *by David L. Good, 1989*

SEASONS OF GRACE: A History of the Catholic Archdiocese of Detroit, *by Leslie Woodcock Tentler, 1990*

THE POTTERY OF JOHN FOSTER: Form and Meaning, *by Gordon and Elizabeth Orear, 1990*

THE DIARY OF BISHOP FREDERIC BARAGA: First Bishop of Marquette, Michigan, *edited by Regis M. Walling and Rev. N. Daniel Rupp, 1990*

WALNUT PICKLES AND WATERMELON CAKE: A Century of Michigan Cooking, *by Larry B. Massie and Priscilla Massie, 1990*

THE MAKING OF MICHIGAN, 1820–1860: A Pioneer Anthology, *edited by Justin L. Kestenbaum, 1990*

AMERICA'S FAVORITE HOMES: A Guide to Popular Early Twentieth-century Homes, *by Robert Schweitzer and Michael W. R. Davis, 1990*

BEYOND THE MODEL T: The Other Ventures of Henry Ford, *by Ford R. Bryan, 1990*

LIFE AFTER THE LINE, *by Josie Kearns, 1990*

MICHIGAN LUMBERTOWNS: Lumbermen and Laborers in Saginaw, Bay City, and Muskegon, 1870–1905, *by Jeremy W. Kilar, 1990*

DETROIT KIDS CATALOG: The Hometown Tourist, *by Ellyce Field, 1990*

WAITING FOR THE NEWS, *by Leo Litwak, 1990 (reprint)*

DETROIT PERSPECTIVES, *edited by Wilma Wood Henrickson, 1991*

LIFE ON THE GREAT LAKES: A Wheelsman's Story, *by Fred W. Dutton, edited by William Donohue Ellis, 1991*

COPPER COUNTRY JOURNAL: The Diary of Schoolmaster Henry Hobart, 1863–1864, *by Henry Hobart, edited by Philip P. Mason, 1991*

JOHN JACOB ASTOR: Business and Finance in the Early Republic, *by John Denis Haeger, 1991*

SURVIVAL AND REGENERATION: Detroit's American Indian Community, *by Edmund J. Danziger, Jr., 1991*

STEAMBOATS AND SAILORS OF THE GREAT LAKES, *by Mark L. Thompson, 1991*

COBB WOULD HAVE CAUGHT IT: The Golden Years of Baseball in Detroit, *by Richard Bak, 1991*

MICHIGAN IN LITERATURE, *by Clarence Andrews, 1992*

UNDER THE INFLUENCE OF WATER: Poems, Essays, and Stories, *by Michael Delp, 1992*

THE COUNTRY KITCHEN, *by Della T. Lutes, 1992 (reprint)*

THE MAKING OF A MINING DISTRICT: Keweenaw Native Copper 1500–1870, *by David J. Krause, 1992*

KIDS CATALOG OF MICHIGAN ADVENTURES, *by Ellyce Field, 1993*

HENRY'S LIEUTENANTS, *by Ford R. Bryan, 1993*

HISTORIC HIGHWAY BRIDGES OF MICHIGAN, *by Charles K. Hyde, 1993*

LAKE ERIE AND LAKE ST. CLAIR HANDBOOK, *by Stanley J. Bolsenga and Charles E. Herndendorf, 1993*

PONTIAC AND THE INDIAN UPRISING, *by Howard H. Peckham, 1994 (reprint)*

CHARTING THE INLAND SEAS: *A History of the U.S. Lake Survey, by Arthur M. Woodford, 1994 (reprint)*

IRON FLEET: The Great Lakes in World War II, *by George J. Joachim, 1994*